Mundidhachel

"Ultimately, this isn't a book about death, but about living filled with wisdom that has been tempered by loss and pain."

—**Donald M. Murray,** author of the column, "Now and Then" in the *Boston Globe*, and the book, *The Lively Shadow—Living With the Death of a Child*

"Robert and Linda Waxler have written a book that is easy and difficult to read. Easy, because they write simply and clearly with graceful references to English literature and the Jewish religion. Difficult, because they make us follow them through the grinding sequences of apprehension as Jonathan moves slowly toward death, then the long journey through the pain of final loss. Their diligence commands our attention."

—**Steven L. Nickman, M.D.,** Psychiatrist at Massachusetts General Hospital and Harvard Medical School and co-editor of *Continuing Bonds: New Understandings of Grief*

"Born not many years before Jonathan, I was struck instantly by the relatedness I felt. The painting for the cover came to mind easily. I was delivered to my own troubled youth, peering through the sparklers, swimming in a deep, slate-colored, Fourth of July night sky. The Waxlers remind us of how difficult it is as youths to communicate when we struggle inside ourselves. Jonathan has left us a tremendous gift to learn from. Thank you, Jonathan. Thank you, Robert and Linda Waxler."

— **Peter Sylvada,** artist, author of cover painting "Cowboy Jonathan"

"Bob and Linda Waxler's courage and willingness to share their story is a gift to all of us who have children at risk. And the truth of their story is that all our children are at risk."

—**David Tebaldi,** Executive Director, *Massachusetts Foundation for the Humanities*

Losing Jonathan

Text © 2003 Robert Waxler, Linda Waxler
All rights reserved.
© Spinner Publications, Inc.
New Bedford, Massachusetts 02740
Printed in the United States of America
Support provided by the Massachusetts Cultural Council.

Cover painting, "Cowboy Jonathan" by Peter Sylvada

Library of Congress Cataloging-in-Publication Data
Waxler, Robert P., 1944-
  Losing Jonathan / by Robert and Linda Waxler.
  p.cm.
  ISBN 0-932027-768 (pbk.)
  1. Waxler, Jonathan Blake, 1969-1995--Death and burial. 2. Narcotics--United
States--Overdosage. 3. Heroin habit--United States. 4. Parent and adult child--
United States. 5. Bereavement--United States. I. Waxler, Linda, 1944-II. Title.
    HV5822.H4W39 2003
    362.29'3'092--dc21
                                    2003008102

Losing Jonathan

Robert Waxler
Linda Waxler

Spinner Publications, Inc.

New Bedford, Massachusetts

To our parents

Felix and Helen Waxler
Fred and Elizabeth Lassoff

Acknowledgments

There are so many wonderful people to thank for making this book possible. Thank you so much. You helped save our lives.

Joanne and Jimmy Gardner, and Judy Morris and Lorne MacHattie, who were with us from the beginning, offering insight from their own pain and loss. Jeff Gardner, John Gardner, Rachel Morris—you will always have a place in our hearts.

And all those early readers, colleagues and friends, who gave us encouragement. We will always appreciate your love and wisdom, especially Howard Senzel, Richard Larschan, Selma Botman, Leo Allen, Jean Trounstine, Anne Diffily, Bob Kane, Bernie Glassman, Bill Kaufman, Raphael Kanter, Earl Grollman, Harold Kushner, Donna Wares, Mike Lannon, Cathy Houser, Mary Hallet, and Evie and David Sarles.

And to all the people, sensitive and caring, at the *Boston Globe Magazine,* the *Providence Journal* and *Brown Magazine* who believed in our work and helped to publish sections of it in early versions.

And special thanks to the team at Spinner Publications: Joe Thomas, visionary publisher, Marsha McCabe, wonderful editor, Andrea Tavares, compassionate administrator, and, of course, Milt George and Jay Avila, super staff.

Finally, we want to thank our son Jeremy for his courage and his strength. You make our hearts smile.

Contents

Introduction

by Donald M. Murray

I grew up in the Pollyanna generation in which we were taught not to speak of the unpleasant. It was not in good taste. But indoors, behind shutters and shades drawn, we spoke of the deaths, diseases, disloyalties, cruelties, and behaviors we tried to keep hidden from the neighbors. We had an elemental need to hear and tell the stories that revealed and explored the human condition.

Few stories are as significant as the death of a child, and we need to hear the stories of those who have suffered our deepest fears. Robert and Linda Waxler tell the story of the long painful loss of their son as he became addicted to the heroin that finally killed him.

They practice the strange kindness of telling their story with honest, specific details. And the more specific they are, the more individual their story, the more universal it becomes.

The magic in storytelling lies in the fact that we tell our personal stories and readers bring their own living to the reading and collaborate in creating the story they need. Each story is different as it is tuned to each reader's life. This book will not only help those who fear drug addiction in our children and their death before us, it will help all of us as we live out our fragile lives.

The storyteller names our fears. That naming is important. Once something, no matter how terrible, is named we can begin to deal with it. The real dragon is better than the imagined one. I learned this in infantry combat and in the loss of a daughter.

A death, even one as terrible and out of proper order as Jonathan Waxler's, can be survived. The father and mother and brother and friends—many in Jonathan's case—have to go on with their living, helping each other and reaching out to strangers.

In reading this book, I retell my own story, and in doing it I reinforce what I have learned, discover new truths and prepare myself for the other losses which are inevitable. To live without knowing how temporary life is, makes our living trivial. There is no true life without death, no light without dark, no hope without despair, no companionship without loneliness.

Ultimately, this isn't a book about death, but about living filled with wisdom that has been tempered by loss and pain. In allowing the book to take them where life takes them—to their other son Jeremy's wedding for example—allows us to celebrate survival and instructs us to love and appreciate what we still have. Paying attention to the significant found in the insignificant becomes a daily memorial service for the children we have lost.

This book is for Jonathan and for each of us.

Donald M. Murray's column, "Now and Then" apppears in the Boston Globe. *He is author of the recently published book,* The Lively Shadow—Living With the Death of a Child, *Ballantine, 2003.*

"A man is up against a hard game
when he has to die to beat it."

— Zora Neale Hurston

"In remembrance lies
the secret of redemption."

— Ba'al Shem Tov

Part One

Cowboy Jonathan

*I*t was always just as the sun began to cast its haunting shadows against the brick buildings in Providence that I would walk across the Brown University campus green in the 1960s and settle into a chair in the John Hay Library. Resting my book on the long wooden table illuminated by a Tiffany-style lamp, I would read the Romantic poets: Wordsworth and Coleridge, Blake and Keats. Through them, I began to understand the importance of literature, how it could make a difference in our lives.

> *The Child is father of the Man;*
> *And I could wish my days to be*
> *Bound each to each by natural piety.*

How old was I when I first came across those lines from Wordsworth? A sophomore, 19 years old?

Nearly 40 years have passed, and I am talking about Wordsworth with a group of undergraduates at the University of Massachusetts at Dartmouth. They look much as I did in my days at Brown. I ask a young man to comment on the poem assigned this autumn day, Wordsworth's story of Michael and his son Luke.

> *Than that a child, more than all other gifts*
> *That earth can offer to declining man,*
> *Brings hope with it, and forward-looking thoughts,*
> *And stirrings of inquietude...*

I want him to tell me about these lines, what he sees in them, what he feels, what he believes. He may not sense the full weight of these lines in the classroom today, but I am convinced he will remember their cadence and eventually come to their meaning.

Like Wordsworth, I know literature can redeem us. It can, at its best, soothe the sting of death itself. A shared story serves as a covenant that binds us together. As Wordsworth's Michael tells his son Luke, as they work together side by side, shortly before Luke goes off into the city never to be seen again:

> 'Twill be between us; but, whatever fate
> Befal thee, I shall love thee to the last,
> And bear thy memory with me to the grave.'

Wordsworth knew the simple dignity of honest labor and the joy of shared memory called forth through the language of the heart. When I read him with my undergraduates today, though, I often silently recall fragments of another story, one he did not know but one he would have appreciated.

It is a story about another young man, my son Jonathan Blake Waxler, whose gravestone stands in a grassy field with other grave markers and quietly reads back to us these dates:

February 9, 1969—August 20, 1995.

Like most fathers, I loved him with a radiance and joy that Wordsworth would have fully understood.

> Then sing ye Birds, sing sing a joyous song!...
>
> We in thought will join your throng
> Ye that pipe and ye that play
> Ye that through your hearts to-day
> Feel the gladness of the May!
> What though the radiance that was once so bright
> Be now for ever taken from my sight.

~

When Jonathan was young, I would make up cowboy stories for him at bedtime long after the sun had gone down. Cowboy Jonathan became a character of endless adventure, riding off to meet his next challenge, returning home weary yet always ready for another journey out. We were never certain what would happen to Cowboy Jonathan when he set out on his ride any particular night, but we cared about him, rooted for him, felt his danger, and celebrated his triumphs. He became part of our collective memory, and we carried with us traces of his story wherever we went.

Cowboy Jonathan lived in a mythical place between father and son, a place that Wordsworth helped to define, a place mixed with memory and desire (as T. S. Eliot said). It is a place that remains as real and significant to me as other locations of shared experience. That is what Wordsworth knew: Literature can give us a place, a habitation, and a name through which to live and dream.

In my imagination now, I am sitting once again at a wooden table in the John Hay Library recalling one of the final times I saw Jonathan. The bright sun catches the curls of his light brown hair, sparkling as he reads a poem to me while we wait patiently for his plane at La Guardia airport in New York. It could have been Wordsworth.

> The Child is father of the Man
> And I could wish my days to be
> Bound each to each by natural piety.

~

Jonathan Blake Waxler was my first son, born in 1969 in a fierce snowstorm in Boston with family surrounding him, dead in 1995 lying on a bed alone in San Francisco with a needle stuck in his vein. That is the starkness of it, but it says nothing about the beauty and truth of the man or the story.

His middle name came from the poet William Blake, a visionary artist who, like Jonathan, celebrated the imagination as life itself. Blake lived a long life, played out his robust potential. Jonathan did not, although in his short life he accomplished more than most achieve through many years. He taught and he wrote, endlessly struggled for those less fortunate than himself, knew more about compassion than anyone else I ever met.

His friends always claimed he had a rare sparkle that could light up a room, a gift from childhood when he would race around our house opening cupboards, exploring new hideouts, exciting everyone with his boundless exuberance. "Energy is Eternal Delight," Blake once wrote, and Jonathan perfectly embodied that fiery aphorism. His hearty laugh could transform an awkward moment into a wonder.

Yet the delight of a sparkler is always short-lived, I suppose, like those slim silver rods I remember when I was young on the Fourth of July, stirring excitement and wonder with their blue sparks electrifying the air and then quickly fizzling and fading into darkness.

The Sparkler

*Y*es, Jonathan Blake, born in a ferocious February blizzard.
"You better bring your wife in early," the doctor told me
on the phone that evening when the labor pains began. "It
should be quite a storm before it's over."

And then Linda and I were off, grabbing the small suitcase already
packed, checking quickly through the apartment, four rooms shaped
like a box in a modern brick building on the outskirts of Boston: Our
bedroom, king-size bed carefully tucked in tight, lamps posed for reading late at night; a smaller bedroom, converted into a study for my work
as a graduate student at Boston College, lovingly caressed now with a
brand-new crib, cushioned layette for changing diapers, several bright
colored mobiles hanging on thin wires dangling from the ceiling; a
living room/dining room combination and a tiny kitchenette with a
refrigerator, brimming with food on every shelf, eagerly awaiting our
return from the hospital with a new infant.

I looked at Linda with my baby-face smile and took her hand gently
in mine, our cheeks warming with anticipation as we headed out the
door to our old blue Chevrolet parked in the back of the building. Her
dark curly hair seemed to dance with excitement in beat with her big
brown eyes.

The snow was already falling, thick flakes on the windshield,
wipers busily sweeping across the glass, as we wound our way from
our working-class neighborhood on River Street in Hyde Park up the
Jamaica Way toward Boston Lying-In in the center of the hospital
district. I drove off the slippery road at least once that night, unable
to see where the street, glazed with snow, ended and the sidewalk in
Jamaica Plain began. But we made it. And late the next afternoon, after
hours and hours of labor, our first son, with a big head and notable
shoulders, arrived.

On February 9, two years from the day that Bob and I had our first date, Jonathan was born, our miracle, our dream. I was not aware it had snowed. I was only aware of the change that had taken place in our lives, that our lives were now almost complete.

I did not have my glasses when he was born and felt I could not see him, this wonder that Bob and I had created. The nurse said, "We can't get you your glasses today, maybe tomorrow, we're so shorthanded because of the storm." But Bob, the new young father, aching to hold his child (fathers were not allowed this privilege in 1969), retrieved the glasses from another room so I could see.

Jonathan was born moving and never stopped. As an infant, any time we held him in our lap his tiny legs locked and he would stand. He cried when we put him back into a seated position. His grandparents said his legs would not develop properly.

He turned over at a very few weeks (we thought it was an accident until it happened again a day or two later) and sat up, stood up, and walked around his crib all in the same week at five months. At eight months, he was walking, and from that time on, the world dragged him into its web, and he explored all of it. We tied, locked, and gated dangerous areas, but he found ways to get in.

We called him our sparkler, and sparkle he did. He wanted to try everything and literally eat up the world. He was wonderful, thoughtful, bright, and kind, but it was difficult to rein him in.

Chavez and Garcia: Protest and Pot

I have always been proud of Jonathan, even after that wretched night of August 20th when he lost the only battle that makes any difference now, his struggle against the insidious monster, heroin.

I never saw the small apartment at 360 Nevada Street in San Francisco, the one he lived in the night he overdosed. But I can picture the room he had during that short period. Jonathan and Steven Johnson, a man in his 40s, got the apartment together after exiting the Henry Ohloff House, a halfway house in the San Francisco hills, hoping that together they might renew their lives with each other's help. Johnson's father was an artist on Block Island, and Johnson himself had been battling an alcohol addiction for several years. I can only wish now that Steven Johnson had been in the apartment to help Jonathan that night.

The little room Jonathan lived in must have had a dresser with his clothes folded neatly in the drawers, a small sense of order set against the chaos of his life, chaos represented most clearly by the drug paraphernalia that rested, I imagine, on the top of the bureau near his tightly made bed when the coroner arrived with his black bag that night. On the walls of that room were two posters. This I know. Johnson told me about those posters in a tearful voice when I spoke to him on the phone a few hours after Jonathan died.

One poster pictured Cesar Chavez, inspiration for Jonathan's ongoing fight for social justice and a democratic society. Jonathan had earned a master's degree in Labor Studies at the University of Massachusetts, Amherst, and worked as an organizer for the United Electrical Workers and various community groups. "Jonathan changed our lives when he helped put together that strike in Albany," workers told Linda and me once at a labor gathering. Like Cesar Chavez, he had taught them something important about dignity and about the determination of the human will, they said.

Next to the poster of Chavez, or perhaps on an adjacent wall, Jonathan had placed a poster of Jerry Garcia, the leader of the Grateful Dead. I am not sure if it was the music or the lifestyle that attracted Jonathan to the Dead; no doubt it was the easy freedom and communal style. When he was very young, he said he wanted to follow the gypsies through Europe, and I suppose following the Grateful Dead had some of that same promise in it.

He wasn't perfect. But who is? There was that time a few years before his death, when his younger brother Jeremy drove up to UMass Amherst in the Pioneer Valley to see a Dead concert with him. Before the music started that day, Jonathan was arrested in the crowd for smoking pot, leaving Jeremy, too innocent then, alone. I was surprised when I heard about it; it seemed out of character for Jonathan to leave his little brother. Jeremy looked up to him, counted on him for advice, knew the warm glow of his affection.

A year later, Jonathan was arrested again, in the Whitmore Administration Building at UMass. It was not pot provoking the authorities this time, though, but principle pushing him forward. In solidarity with a dedicated group of rebellious students, he was dragged away late at night, into district court the next morning before a judge in dark robes, for protesting military research on the Amherst campus.

Jonathan was more Ken Kesey than Ozzy Osbourne; more Bob Dylan than Heavy Metal; more Easy Rider than Hells Angels. He was closer to the shtetl than to the wild wild west, closer to I. B. Singer than to Norman Mailer. He was gentle, a kind and generous offshoot of the 60s.

In the end, though, Garcia died in a drug rehabilitation center only ten days or so before Jonathan. Chavez died a couple of years earlier, in 1993. Jonathan admired these men; he had shaped his life with them in mind.

A Grave and a Bris: Death and Birth

*J*onathan has been dead for over six years. He would be 32 years old, although I always think of him now at the age of 26. I visited his grave recently and could recall vividly that cold day in August we put him in the ground. It was a private burial, a few family members, chilled with grief. I lingered by the grave that summer day, drawn to the plain pine casket in the ground, as the others quietly moved away. Finally someone touched my arm, as if to shake me from a spell, hoping I would follow the rest out of the cemetery. But I was fixed to the spot where I stood. It was fortunate; otherwise I would have stepped with Jonathan at that moment into the silence of the tomb.

It is a commonplace that children should not die before their parents, that there is something unnatural about it, that it works against the order of the generations. When Jonathan died, part of my future died. His death is my loss, the breaking of a bond between father and son, the end of a promise and a dream. Yet he still lives in memory, thrills me with his resounding laugh, his voracious appetite centered in the belly of life.

I have always believed that the central rhythm in this life is death and birth, sorrow and joy. That natural cadence gives us the self-conscious understanding of our sensuous bodies, reminds us of our mortality. My favorite poet, William Blake, knew this well. Fear plus hope equals vision, he wrote in his journal, expressing his conviction that death and birth could be transformed by the power of the Romantic imagination. Blake's vision is difficult to grasp, but his attention to the haunting rhythm of death and birth resonates with me. Although Jonathan's corpse lies silent in the grave, a whisper rustles through the imagination of all those who care about him.

~

Yes, the earth seems saturated with death these days, but a good friend of Jonathan's had a bris for his eight-day-old son recently at his parents' home around the corner from where we live. He named the baby after his favorite great uncle and for Jonathan, two men who loved life, two men he would always remember, as he put it, after the rabbi clipped the infant's foreskin and offered the ritual blessings.

"How could anyone who knew Jonathan ever forget him?" his good friend said after the ceremony was over, clearly longing for his return. Linda and I stood together listening intently, our bagels and cream cheese balanced on plain white paper plates carefully held in our hands.

"Jonathan had so many friends," this proud new father told us. "He was like a hub holding all the diverse spokes together. When we lost him, we lost our center. Jonathan knew everyone, and everyone knew him.

"I remember Jonathan calling me up at Colby one cold winter day. He had a couple of last-minute tickets to a Phish concert in the small auditorium over at Smith College for the next night. Jonathan knew I loved that band. So there we were in the balcony that night, and Jonathan starts yelling down to the band between songs, 'Hey, it's my birthday coming up. Play the antelope song for me,' he shouts out. Then the lead singer looks up at us. 'OK Waxler, we hear you,' he says. 'This one is for Waxler up there in the balcony.' I am amazed. And everyone else in the auditorium must have been too. That was Jonathan. He brought magic with him."

Yes, for me the naming of a new child that afternoon in our neighborhood was a touching moment in praise of Jonathan, and a startling reminder of the covenant sealed in the flesh of the organs of Jewish generations. But there was also a murmur there, disturbing the silence of Jonathan's grave. Evoking Jonathan's name linked the living with the dead, connected the circumcision of a newborn with the burial of a corpse. It was a moment of vision, bringing an end to the week, a typical week, filled with the rhythm of death and birth, an extraordinary week, a baby taking on the flesh of Jonathan's future.

I traveled back through the cadence to Jonathan's grave, to William Blake and to Wordsworth:

> Surprised by joy—impatient as the Wind
> I turned to share the transport—Oh! with whom
> But Thee, deep buried in the silent tomb,
> That spot which no vicissitude can find?
> Love, faithful love, recalled thee to my mind—
> But how could I forget thee? Through what power,
> Even for the least division of an hour,
> Have I been so beguiled as to be blind
> To my most grievous loss?—That thought's return
> Was the worst pang that sorrow ever bore,
> Save one, one only, when I stood forlorn,
> Knowing my heart's best treasure was no more;
> That neither present time, nor years unborn
> Could to my sight that heavenly face restore.

Washington and the Fir Trees

*H*ow is it possible that we missed the signs of menace emanating from this sparkler, this brilliant son of ours? He seemed so interested, so enthusiastic about everything. He could talk about the great works of literature with an adult sophistication, had traveled the world with his maternal grandparents when most of his friends had barely left the neighborhood. He was like a scholar gypsy seeking adventure.

When his younger brother was born in St. Charles hospital in Port Jefferson, Long Island, on a sweltering summer day in July of 1974, Jonathan stayed in the Holiday Inn overnight with Linda's parents. "He found some matches in the room," his grandmother told us the next day. "Started a small fire in the bathroom." It wasn't rage or jealousy that motivated him, though. Just curiosity, a restlessness. The five-year-old needed to know what matches could do.

Linda, trained as a young, dedicated public school teacher, was finishing up her master's degree at Stony Brook then; I was completing my doctorate degree in English. We were happy, a normal family, not much money, filled with ideals, two sons, on the go.

We all flew out to Walla Walla, Washington six weeks after Jeremy was born so I could work on my dissertation, the early works of Blake, and teach for a year at Whitman College, a small liberal arts school with an Ivy League reputation among the wealthy wheat farmers near the Idaho border. When we returned East to Massachusetts at the end of that academic year, we were returning home, to New Bedford, where I had grown up and where my parents and brother still lived in the West End, a pleasant middle-class neighborhood. I felt deeply committed to the area and believed, as I still do, that it was a wonderful place to raise a family.

New Bedford, located in the southeastern corner of the state, near the ocean, had been a famous whaling town in the nineteenth century, now a fishing port with wonderful ethnic neighborhoods, narrow streets, historic houses. My roots are there, near Buttonwood Park, a sprawling and open space with green grass, baseball fields, flower gardens, woods with old maple trees, a pond often frozen in winter for ice skating, even a zoo. With its three-decker tenements and tired textile mills, sections of the city often seemed gritty, of another generation; but there was a quiet and proud beauty throughout the city that whispered of the promise of the American dream, of what the future could bring if we could only hear it mingling with the roar of the ocean waves.

I had been hired as an assistant professor in the English department at Southeastern Massachusetts University, later to become part of the University of Massachusetts, in Dartmouth, a suburb just over the border from New Bedford. SMU was the only university south of Boston, and many of its students came from working-class homes, the first in their families to attend college. It was an exciting opportunity for me to use my education to contribute to a community I already felt close to.

When we got settled, Linda decided to stay home with Jeremy during the day, teaching math part-time in the evenings at Fisher Junior College. Jonathan enrolled in the first-grade at Pulaski School in New Bedford.

He was energetic that year, excited, kept jumping up from his chair in class, talking to his classmates, not paying much attention to his lessons. His teacher wanted him out, thought he lacked focus, called the guidance counselor in.

The guidance counselor turned out to be Mrs. Jackson, one of those wise women from a previous generation deeply committed to the dream of public education.

"Well, Jonathan, how did you like it down there in the nation's capital?" she asked the six-year-old when he came to her office.

"Mrs. Jackson," Jonathan replied without hesitation in a clear and gentle tone. "There are two Washingtons in this country. The national capital and the state of Washington. I lived in the state of Washington."

"I'm very impressed by Jonathan," she told us later. "And the scores on the tests I gave him confirm my belief. He's a very smart boy, and a gentleman."

"Jonathan is probably bored in your class," Mrs. Jackson suggested to his first grade teacher. "You need to give him more challenging work." And the teacher did just that, eventually making Jonathan one of her favorite students through first and second grades.

He had a charm.

~

Jonathan was the first one in our family to see Jeremy walk. "Come quick," Jonathan shouted one bright morning from the living room in our apartment in New Bedford. "I was holding his hands in front of me, and then I let him go. He took a step toward me, and then he fell. I know he'll get up again. Come quick," he insisted.

My side of the family always agreed, especially when we were standing close together at family gatherings in New Bedford: "Jonathan looks more like you, Bob, than like Linda." Linda's family also agreed, at least among themselves. "He looks just like you, Linda," they would say when we drove down to their home in Connecticut for a cookout on the neatly cropped lawns in their sprawling backyard in suburban West Hartford.

Jonathan played Little League baseball on the dirt diamonds around town in those days, sat amazed at his first sight of the Green Monster in left field at Fenway Park, followed Yastrzemski's every move from the owner's box just above the Red Sox dugout, hated the damn Yankees with a passion.

He was not beyond a fight when it was demanded, like the time he beat up Mike, our next-door neighbor, a boy a year older than he was. Michael had picked on Jeremy, half his size, once too often. Jonathan saw Michael in the front yard, ran over to him, taught him a lesson.

Jonathan took his first trip abroad with Linda's parents when he was ten. "We went to Westminster Abbey," his grandmother told us. "It was closed for the day when we got there. He was so disappointed, but he never gave up. He needed to get in that place, and that was that. So he looked all around the grounds outside of the abbey until he found what he was looking for, a caretaker with a key, a man to serve his purpose. 'I have to get in,' Jonathan told him. 'It's very important. I have to see the Poet's Corner where Blake's buried. My father's a Blake scholar,' he explained to the caretaker. So the man unlocked the front door and let him roam around. Jonathan headed right for that corner."

He attended Hebrew School in the late afternoons and on the weekends. At his bar-mitzvah, he chanted the Haftarah, led the congregation in prayer, and talked about the importance of *tikkun olam*, the repairing of the world. And he prayed at the High Holiday services each year with the rest of the family.

He enjoyed freshman football, took honors courses, was elected co-captain of the golf team. Hung out at Allendale, the local country club. Worked hard as a caddy.

As smart as Jonathan was, though, it was really his kindness that made him stand out, that drew people to him. He was a loyal brother and friend, always seeking people willing to share that sense of compassion. He thought nothing about the honors he received—the Quill and Scroll Award for superior achievement in high school journalism, his school letter for outstanding work throwing the shot put—all such honors seemed to be fleeting moments for him, far from the essential rhythm of the human heart.

Yes, he had so many good friends. In high school he seemed serious about Cindy one year. She was bright and attractive, devoted to him. They were always laughing together, her long black hair dancing in the air.

When Linda and I came home late on a Saturday night, the two of them were usually downstairs in the dark. Just finishing up watching the latest video, they would always claim, as we heard the rustling on the couch, the clothes tucked back in, the light switch clicking on.

Jonathan was, in other words, like any young man his age, a normal kid romping through the public school corridors of life, enjoying a party. But he was serious and philosophical too, and the importance of community became part of his growing vision. At 17, he spent a summer in Israel, writing an article for the International USY (United Synagogue Youth) magazine when he returned:

> ...On the kibbutz, guards patrolled the area throughout the night, on alert for possible terrorist attacks. But each morning I would get out of bed at sunrise to go to work as part of a team picking potatoes in the fields. We would not think of the terrorists or the armed guards, but sing songs together to forget the brutal heat and the difficult work. We were a family helping each other, sharing common values and goals. And I was learning how to be a man, how to contribute my energy in a communal effort.

He was learning then, as he always was, "how to be a man," as he said, a man who felt the depth of a self joined to a difficult history, a depth that makes us more than mere surfaces. As he put it later in that same article, thinking about his engagement with the significant markers of a people:

> ...these landmarks and the realization that I was surrounded by thousands of Jews gave me a sense of belonging to a history that was deeply embedded within me. At the Wailing Wall, I stood with 12 of my friends and cried for half an hour, thinking about the pain and suffering of Jews throughout the ages...

Yes, I talked with him in my small study when he was still in high school concerning reports I had heard about his use of pot. We often talked. But I saw drugs then through the smoke and haze of the 1960s, not as killers. Only later, much later, would I realize the drug culture had changed, that it was now like driving 90 miles an hour blindfolded. Who wouldn't fear that?

Dear Jonathan,

We miss you so much.... Now that it is spring, I think often about when you tried out for the baseball team in New Bedford. You worked so hard and went back over and over while they were trying to decide between the last few kids. Well, you made it because you were determined—not because you were a great player—and you did that so many times in your short life. There was the time that Mrs. Carter let you play in the piano competition even though you did not meet the age requirements. Also, when you made it into the school-wide chorus at Pulaski School even though again you were much too young. You were sure that you should be in it so you simply went to the tryouts. I don't know why that same determination did not win out in your struggle over drugs. Jonathan, we loved you so much and I don't think I will ever truly accept that you are gone. You will always be my son.

Love, Mom

~

One summer, still in high school, Jonathan planted nine small fir trees in the backyard of our raised ranch on Strathmore Road in suburban North Dartmouth, where we moved after I got tenure and a promotion and Linda began teaching again. Those trees have grown from small saplings, two feet tall, to majestic treasures, stretching heavenward a good 20 feet. I often think his spirit is there in the evergreen trees and in the rosebushes he planted for Linda on Mother's Day one year.

He worked as a landscaper on a tree farm that summer, always smiling when he came home at the end of a long day with his dungarees and work shirt caked with dirt.

"Wouldn't it be wonderful to plant some trees there at the edge of the lawn?" we mused one evening around the dinner table.

"Sure, I could do that," Jonathan quickly responded, happy to be of help.

During the Fourth of July weekend, he borrowed a small panel truck and brought those nine fir trees home. And there he was, taking the trees out of the back of the truck, lining them up carefully in a row in the backyard.

It took him a few hours to dig the small holes with the steel shovel, place the trees in the rounded-out plots of ground, cover their roots firmly with the dirt, pack it all down gently. When he was finished, he stood looking at his work, proud, beaming. And those trees stand so tall today, forever pointing to the sky.

He loved to fish and hike. That was how he defined his difference from us, I suppose. He loved nature, growing up in a family that never went camping, that never believed Jews were outdoor people. He would talk about the fly-fishing scenes in Robert Redford's film *A River Runs Through It* with an affection and empathy that revealed a sense of profound serenity and joy. He understood the spiritual bond the two brothers in that film shared casting for trout, knee deep in the rushing waters of the Big Black Foot River, just as he understood the mythic vision dug deep in the bean field Thoreau worked near his cabin in the woods at Walden Pond.

The day after his funeral, I wanted to drive out to his grave. I was desperate to speak with him at least one more time. "You shouldn't go," Linda said. "You can talk to him near those trees in the backyard."

I didn't go out to the cemetery that week, although I did walk near those nine fir trees at the edge of our lawn one morning, telling him I loved him very much, hoping he could hear me, that he had found comfort there.

Heroin

When Linda and I drove him to his dormitory in Amherst for the first week of college, Jonathan had a bright future about him. He stood tall, almost six feet, 180 pounds or so, articulate, handsome.

In those days, he moved in packs, ten girls and ten guys at a dinner party, loads of vegetarian dishes, wine, and good conversation around the table. They all seemed to live together in the same dorms, with ratty clothes, Grateful Dead music in the background. They were the new hippies, anti-fraternity, anti-sorority, anti-establishment. They majored in multidisciplinary subjects like Social Thought and Political Economy, loved Marxist analysis, determined to stay out of the corrupt mainstream.

Jonathan often seemed drawn to girls with names like Wyoming, girls who loved nature, who wanted to be close to him, confide in him, even take care of him at times, like the two who moved out to White Fish, Montana, after college and later pleaded with him to come live with them while he recovered from his addiction.

For a while in college, he was taken by a girl he didn't want to tell us much about. He liked her a lot, had a special respect for her. They both seemed serious about each other, but he wouldn't give us many details.

"I'm going to her house to meet her parents over the vacation," he told us.

"How did it go?" we asked when he returned after the winter break.

"Fine," he said, "just fine."

But it turned out her father was a Lutheran minister. Jonathan had been hesitant to say much about that. He thought we might not approve, I suppose, because she wasn't Jewish. Eventually they drifted apart without regrets.

Yes, his friends were all smart with good hearts, the bright future looking for an alternative.

After four years as an undergraduate, he was awarded his bachelor's degree. Two years later, he had his master's degree. He was on track, we thought.

When he got his job with the United Electrical Workers after finishing his graduate studies at Amherst, we set up a small, two-room apartment for him in an elegant old stone building near the SUNY, Albany campus. We bought him an Oriental-style rug, a new double bed, a few furnishings from BJ's, boosted him through the transition to the next smooth stage of his adult life. It was the nicest and cleanest place he had lived in since leaving home for college.

The first paragraph of the letter Jonathan wrote for his job at the UE captures his hopes and vision at the time. It's dated January 11, 1993.

> In the preamble to the UE Constitution, it speaks of "rank and file control" and promises to "pursue at all times a policy of aggressive struggle to improve our conditions." When the UE separated itself from the CIO in 1949, it proved that it was an organization committed to the betterment of the working class across industrial lines, regardless of race and gender, and that it was not afraid to stand up for its membership's rights. It is this commitment to workers' rights and the creation of a truly democratic society that has drawn me into the labor movement.

Jonathan worked for the UE in Albany for about six months, focusing primarily on helping to organize a successful strike for the electrical workers. Near the end of that short period, the union leaders asked him to move to Pittsburgh, where their headquarters were located. They wanted to use his talent there. But Jonathan claimed he was growing disenchanted with the UE, preferred to stay near the coast, perhaps even New York City. I called an old friend of mine who was working for the Teamsters in Washington, D.C., and asked him if he could help out.

"Well, we could put Jonathan on this research project in New York," he said. "It's only for a few weeks, but it's intriguing work, investigating corruption in the ranks. It could lead to something permanent. But it might not."

So Jonathan decided to pursue the chance and go to New York.

There had been all sorts of young people in the neighborhood in Albany, energetic students, professional go-getters, fertile ground for Jonathan to grow and flourish. He didn't make contact with any of these new people, though—we didn't know why. But Linda and I still didn't suspect much out of the ordinary then. The new job in New York might be temporary, but it appeared to be another solid start.

We thought we were all on track.

~

It happened shortly after Jonathan arrived in New York City. On a Sunday morning, Linda and I received a call from the mother of a friend of Jonathan's in Amherst, her voice breaking, disturbed and embarrassed about what she had to report. Jonathan was using heroin. It was a terrible shock, difficult to believe. The word "heroin" associated with Jonathan was impossible to accept that day, although the word carved itself into our flesh down to the bone.

After that harrowing call, we phoned Jonathan and told him we wanted to meet him in Amherst. He needed to pack the belongings he had left behind there—stored in a ramshackle apartment above a garage owned by one of his friends. And we wanted to ask him about what we'd heard. Linda and I drove across the state saying little, apprehensive and tense, hoping—it was such a humid July day—that what we feared wasn't true.

We were all perspiring, sweat soaking through our clothes, as we chatted in that sweltering apartment about his new job. Later, we helped him carry some of his clothes down the narrow staircase to his car. It was then that I first noticed it, his arms, black and blue just below the elbows, on the inside, raw and swollen. I had never seen the arms of a heroin addict before, but it was difficult not to believe I was looking at them then.

Jonathan had almost always worn long-sleeve shirts down to his wrists the last year or so. Why he was wearing a short-sleeve shirt on this day I'll never know. Maybe he wanted us to notice his wounded arms. Perhaps it was simply too hot to care.

"Jonathan, what are those bruises on your arms?" I calmly asked him in the midst of the oppressive heat that day. "They look like they could be from heroin."

"Oh, that's nothing," Jonathan replied with a certain insistence. "A window slammed down on them when I was helping my friend John paint his house. They'll be fine in a couple of days," he assured me.

The story was so absurd even Jonathan would chuckle thinking about it a few months later in one of his better moments in recovery. But I must have wanted to believe it at the time, because although I challenged him on it several times that day, I finally accepted his story. Yes, he had used heroin in the past, but he was not using it now, and he had not used it in the last few weeks.

I think Jonathan wanted to tell us about his addiction that day, at least part of him wanted to come home with us, clean the toxins out of his body, start over. But part of him craved for heroin, and that part craved a life different from ours, a gypsy life of sorts, a life far removed from the shelter of middle-class existence, far removed from that "life of quiet desperation" Thoreau warned all of us about so long ago.

"Not possible," I responded when Bob hung up the phone and reported that Jonathan might be using heroin. "Not in our family. Never in families like ours. She's wrong. I'm sure she meant well, but she's wrong." My heart was racing and I felt sick in the pit of my stomach. I could never handle anything like this, so it could not be true.

As we drove to Amherst, I convinced myself that Jonathan would be able to explain the entire misunderstanding and on the return trip things would be back to normal. Of course, they weren't.

Part Two

Entering Hell

S oon after we saw Jonathan in Amherst, we began to hear new reports from some of Linda's relatives that he was acting strangely in New York, shaking and in a cold sweat. So we called him again. Jonathan always called back. We could count on it. I told him I was driving down to New York to see him and find out what was going on. He didn't object. He rarely did.

So began the first of a long series of journeys in pursuit of Jonathan, the young man we were no longer sure of, the young man we constantly feared losing, the young man we could not recognize, the normal young man on the stairs who was no longer there.

I arrived in New York City that Friday around noon and went directly to the Teamsters' office where Jonathan was working, on the East Side around 2nd Avenue and 60th Street. I took an elevator up about five floors near the top of the old crusty building, then walked through a series of rooms that made up the union office. It was typical labor, gray and dedicated. Phones everywhere. Staff busy at old desks. Posters advocating workers' rights. No rugs on the floors, just sawdust and wood.

Jonathan worked by himself in a narrow room in the back with a long table and a phone. His papers, as always, were neatly arranged in organized piles. His sport coat and tie hung on a hook in the corner. "In case I need to go downtown to check court records," he said.

The job was temporary and fragile, like his life at this point, and without the job he would be running out of money within a few days. He didn't have any permanent place to live either.

He took me to his favorite hamburger joint for lunch, a few blocks from his office. "These are the best burgers in New York," he told me with such a persuasive tone that I was sure he was right.

"Jonathan, Mom and I are worried about you," I told him as we ate our burgers, juice dripping off the bun that day. "We've heard that you've been acting strangely. Sweating, dozing off."

"Well, I'm not taking heroin," he insisted. "Those people don't know what they're seeing."

After lunch, we called a psychologist and drug counselor, Larry Barnett, for an appointment. Barnett had been recommended by a psychiatrist, Dr. Fine, who had been helping Jonathan for a few weeks and who had told Linda and me he was optimistic about Jonathan's future, assuring us Jonathan was not currently taking drugs. Dr. Fine would not be the last expert fooled by Jonathan's behavior.

Barnett couldn't meet with us until the next day, so we checked into the local Sheraton Hotel, went to the Carnegie Deli for a pastrami on rye—always an important ritual for us in New York—and then we walked the neon-lit avenues, glancing through the glass windows at the hi-tech equipment in the stores around Broadway. The streets were electric, teeming with people, and I felt Jonathan pulling away from me as we moved.

He was restless and, in retrospect, beginning to suffer some withdrawal. He wanted to be free if he could figure out how to do it, although he never did that night.

A stretch limo pulled next to the curb as we wandered through the crowd around ten that evening. A young driver got out, talked briefly to a small group of people on the street, asking them if they wanted to ride around town. A few got in. The whole scene seemed odd to me, dream-like.

"Don't you think that's a little strange?" I asked Jonathan as we watched the limo pull away.

"They're just having fun," he responded.

I sensed he wanted to go with them. He wanted to break from that little dungeon he found himself in, break from the control of a father desperately trying to protect a son, the control of a judge who might restrict him. He was a young man who desired to laugh and to play, to wander in the wilderness.

We finally went up to our hotel room at the Sheraton. It was a ghostly night: Jonathan gurgling deep down in his lungs as he slept, getting up, going to the bathroom, gagging in muffled tones. In the morning I asked him if he felt all right.

"Just getting over a bad cold," he claimed nonchalantly.

He must have been at the beginning of withdrawal, taking the little heroin he had in small doses then, chipping away at it, trying to preserve some until he could get away from me, get downtown, and somehow make another buy.

"Jonathan should go into a 28-day program immediately," Barnett recommended as we sat later that morning around the desk in his office, one of many rooms in a suite on the Upper West Side. "He's at considerable risk."

"I don't need that," Jonathan quickly replied.

At the time, I couldn't accept the idea either.

We talked and we talked in the office that day, eventually agreeing that Jonathan should start an intensive outpatient program on Monday, but he would first have to be tested to make sure he wasn't taking any drugs. If he failed, he would enter an inpatient program. Jonathan was convincing, and I thought we had all arrived at a reasonable plan. I still naively believed we were all born innocent. Through reason we could win out over the most devilish problems.

"I'll be fine, Dad," Jonathan told me as we walked back to the car together. "You should head home. Make sure Mom is all right."

He had been staying with a union associate in Queens whose wife worked out of town during the week. When she returned on weekends, he had to find another place to stay. He mentioned an inexpensive motel in a Queens neighborhood he was familiar with, and I agreed to pay. I assumed he would start Barnett's outpatient program and return to his friend's apartment on Monday.

As we drove from Manhattan, I spoke to Jonathan about his drug problem, explaining how much I wanted to help him, how special he was to Linda and me.

"Mom and I love you, Jonathan," I told him as I gripped the wheel of the car. "We'd do anything for you."

I saw tears in his eyes as he quietly listened, sitting silently next to me, nodding with recognition. It was the first time I noticed that kind of vulnerability. Perhaps he wanted to say something more at that moment, but he didn't, and neither did I.

~

The motel in Queens didn't look as run-down as I had originally imagined, judging at least from the appearance of the lobby. It was small and dingy, seedy, but not as bad as one might suspect. It had only a single clerk at the desk and a very young Hispanic couple, just married, sitting close together on a couch in the lounge.

With a second glance, though, I thought we might have entered Hell.

Before paying for the room, I wanted to call Linda, explain to her what we were doing, get her perspective. Jonathan was agitated and uncertain, and I was in territory I knew nothing about, unexplored terrain with no guideposts or directions. From a pay phone in the lobby, I dialed home and we both spoke to her and Jeremy. In the middle of the conversation, as if by revelation, Jeremy made clear what we needed to do:

"Don't leave Jonathan in that hotel," Jeremy demanded through the phone. "You have to stay with him."

The tone in Jeremy's voice startled me. He had been home on that Sunday when we received the warning call from the mother of Jonathan's friend, so he was well aware of the situation. He sensed the danger and, in retrospect, seems to have had a better grasp of the moment than Linda and I did. He was a college student himself, had seen his own friends taking drugs at campus parties, and although he had kept his distance, he knew the scene. He was worried about Jonathan, wanted his big brother safe and secure.

Jeremy, five and a half years younger than Jonathan, had always loved to be near him, whether sitting in the backseat of our car on long trips, playing games together as we rolled along those endless stretches of highway, or getting ready for bed in motel rooms late at night as we headed to Disney World in Orlando. Jeremy always felt it was a privilege to be close to Jonathan, to watch him, to be part of his life. Just to sit in front of the television with Jonathan, the two of them together, was always a treat for Jeremy, a moment of brotherhood and fun, especially when free from the eyes of parents for a while.

I couldn't ignore Jeremy's demand, and so turning to Jonathan I asked him again if he was still on heroin. "No, I'm not," he insisted. "Absolutely not."

Then he was on the phone, talking to Linda. I couldn't hear what they were saying. Suddenly he gave the phone back to me.

"Ask him what he just whispered to me," Linda shouted over the phone. "Ask him."

I didn't know what she meant. "Ask him what?"

"Have him tell you what he just told me, that he's still taking heroin."

I looked at Jonathan, standing next to me, hovering over the phone, straining to hear the conversation: "Did you just tell Mom that you're still on heroin?" I asked.

"No, I didn't," he replied.

I couldn't understand what was going on. He talked again to Linda.

And then, turning to me, in a muffled tone he blurted it out: "Yes, I am. I'm still taking heroin."

Uneducated about the drug culture, I felt lost. Jonathan seemed frightened too, as if we were both unaware of how soon or how terrible his withdrawal would be.

"I'm worried about withdrawal," Jonathan told me in that hell pit of a lobby. "I've heard about cases of people dying in such circumstances. I've probably only got about five hours before I get very sick."

Since I had no reason not to believe him, I did.

I made several calls to his doctors, but it was late into the weekend, and so I finally decided to drive back near our home in Massachusetts, imagining if his symptoms got very bad we could stop along the way and check into the emergency ward of the closest hospital.

"Sit down here on the couch for a minute," I said to him then, trying to compose myself and, at the same time, reassure him everything would be all right. "I'm so glad you finally told us about all this, Jonathan. I know how difficult it must be."

Men are not supposed to cry, but we both did in that hotel lobby, from relief perhaps but also from the overwhelming weight of the moment. How had this happened—two well-educated people from a good family, uncertain of their footing, filled with fear and dread, wrestling with the demons of heroin addiction?

I phoned Linda again before we left, telling her about my plan to drive Jonathan near our home in Dartmouth. "Try to find a place where I can take Jonathan when I get close," I urged her. "And call my brother David. He'll help."

For those familiar with the intricacies of drug addiction, this may not have been such a crisis, but as we left New York I was convinced we were now embarked on a life-and-death journey. Over six years have passed since that day, and I realize now that my immediate fears about the severity of his withdrawal were unfounded. I know more about drug addiction now than I could have possibly imagined then. I even bought a phone for my car in case of emergencies. Yet that drive from New York was the beginning of a journey to death. It would change all our lives forever.

A Terrible Virus

*L*ater, much later, we would read about the large number of people dying from heroin sold in the neighborhood where Jonathan had been buying his drugs. We would learn that this "killer heroin" (labeled such even on the bags) was distributed regularly, like a religious ritual, in the stores and streets down in the Greenwich Village area, places Jonathan knew like the veins in his arm.

It is clear now, although it wasn't then, that Jonathan didn't fear the terrible forces out there. And he was out so far. He must have believed he could master these powerful teeming rhythms, just as he believed he could master that brutal chemical—that monster variously known as Slick, Black Tar, Chocolate, Hero, Horse, Mud, Smack, H, Skag, Junk—heroin itself.

Jonathan had always been a namer of names, a master of words and signs, a good reader, a semiologist controlling what he perceived as the meaning lurking beneath the flickering surfaces of life. In high school he had once gone with his Hebrew school class on a bus trip to Boston. At the time, he was reading *The Chosen* by Chaim Potok, a novel about two orthodox Jewish boys, good friends, Little League baseball players, and deep readers, but with very different views of the modern world.

"I got into a conversation about that novel with Jonathan while we were on the bus," the Hebrew school principal told me. "It was a pleasure listening to Jonathan talk about the characters. His ideas were mature, sophisticated. I rarely have such stimulating discussions, even with adults."

Yes, Jonathan sparkled, and it was perhaps that brilliance that made him believe he could master anything, that swelling of confidence and overweening pride that convinced him he could enter deep into the dark side of himself, the pleasure and the horror of it, that he could confront it, name it and give it a shape, give it his own spin and control.

I would like to know what he was thinking then, how deep he actually journeyed, what he was looking for, what he might have found.

But in the end it was most likely only the abyss that he discovered, an empty space filled by a chemical and nothing more, a physiological disease that finally killed him like a terrible virus. Perhaps the rush of heroin running through his veins was the only sign he had left of the vitality of life, the fire he had once known turned to the ennui of addiction, the sickness of a life so close to death.

Jonathan once claimed we didn't understand the thrill of knowing the danger of "killer heroin." Was this bravado? He had a great passion for life, that I know. He loved to be traveling, on the road, moving, mobile. He certainly didn't want to get stuck. I know he never gave up. He didn't want to break our hearts.

Yes, I wish I could talk to him now, tell him I am not angry at him, that I would never be ashamed of him, that all I ever wanted was for him to return home. I wanted him whole, not the ghost but the man. After hearing a song by the Eagles on the radio once, I wrote him: "Oh desperado, let somebody love you before it's too late." I know he knew how much we loved him, but once he was addicted he couldn't let that love in.

Was he like Wordsworth's chosen son, the Pedlar who "in all shapes found a secret and mysterious soul, a fragrance and a spirit of strange meaning"? Or was he in the end someone who had simply lost his way, grasping for the superficial surface of things, "the outside marks by which society has parted man from man, neglectful of the universal heart"?

I want to know why.

Finding a Safe Place: Butler Hospital

*A*s we left New York on that miserable day in the mid-summer of 1994, Jonathan was sick, vomiting a little by the side of the car, looking very pale.

"Maybe we should go to a dealer," he suggested. "Just to get enough heroin to ease the pain of withdrawal."

I almost agreed, believing he knew more about all this than I did. In the end, though, I refused to take him, knowing somehow that the idea was haunted.

"I'm not going to do that, Jonathan," I told him. He didn't argue.

I finally helped him into the backseat of the car, covered him with a spare blanket from the trunk, and began that lonely trip toward home.

Jonathan dozed off, waking up whenever I stopped at a pay phone to call Linda to see if she and David had found a bed for him. He couldn't eat along the way, although he grew thirsty, his mouth parched. I bought him a soda at a rest stop on the Connecticut Turnpike and watched him take a few slow sips from the same kind of giant cup he once loved to gulp from when he was healthy and fully alive. I wanted to chat with him, as we often did, about politics and current events, recent films and videos, but it would have to be another day, I thought, a day when he was laughing again, a day when he had regained his footing in this world, a day when he was no longer floating like a ghost in another place. I was frightened, but convinced he would recover. It was impossible to imagine anything else.

I checked in with Linda and David every hour at pay phones en route. They were having problems finding a hospital for Jonathan. Many of the local medical centers didn't take detox patients, and all the beds in the detox units were filled. As we approached the Rhode Island border, I kept wondering how much time we had before Jonathan went into full withdrawal and couldn't imagine what would happen if we didn't find a safe haven for him. Finally Linda and David made contact with

Butler Hospital in Providence, less than an hour's drive from our home in Massachusetts. After a telephone battle about the insurance, Butler agreed to admit Jonathan.

It was dark when I entered Providence with Jonathan sleeping in the back seat of my Toyota Camry. I remembered Butler only vaguely from my undergraduate days at Brown, when some of my friends had served as student interns at this mental hospital with its well-cropped green grass and flowering trees that made it seem like a college campus, serene and pastoral on the outside, but menacing on the inside, haunted by the demons of the unconscious.

> *I think often about the year before Jonathan died when Bob had to go rescue him during his frequent relapses. I stayed home, numb and scared, waiting for Bob's calls and instructions on what I might do from my end. I cannot remember ever feeling so helpless. There should be some help out there for people who are experiencing this and I hope that someday I can help someone in this situation. Maybe it would have been better to let him fall down, deep into a hole, but how can a parent do that?*

~

Butler Hospital was the first of many institutions Jonathan would go to over the next year, from detox centers to inpatient programs to medical hospitals to halfway houses. Filled with people who often cared, they were nevertheless institutions, part of a bureaucracy I have grown to despise in the same way I despise every dehumanizing process that seems to harden the human heart in the name of efficiency and control. They had plans and they had methods. They had programs and they had strategies. Indeed, during the year Jonathan experienced a full range of recovery-community options. "Why don't you write a book about these places?" I once suggested to him half-jokingly. "A Baedecker, a travel guide. You could rate the various spots in the recovery community across the United States."

I am not bitter about these places. I think they can often be helpful. But even the best of them remind me of jails, places robbed of the human heartbeat, clichés that have no vitality. If you are fortunate, you will leave them and decide to live a normal life. You will have grown sick and tired of the chatter.

I drove in the dark onto the grounds of Butler, found the main building stripped of staff and desolate on this late Saturday night, and immediately started talking to the first person I saw.

"Jonathan needs to get settled right away," I insisted. "Before he goes into full withdrawal."

The pleasant middle-aged woman in charge of admissions responded calmly from behind the counter, handed me two forms to fill out, expressed some mild concern about the insurance, and assured us: "A doctor will be with you soon."

We were brought to a separate room to wait, one of those old spacious physician's offices with comfortable furniture and shelves lined with medical books. I covered Jonathan again with a blanket as he dozed on the old brown-leather couch.

A half-hour later the doctor came in, friendly and sympathetic, asked a series of routine questions, examined Jonathan carefully with his stethoscope and tongue depressor, and then explained that Jonathan would be brought up to the detox floor and watched closely during the night. I wanted to go with him, but that was against the rules. I was convinced Jonathan was about to experience a terrible time in withdrawal. I wanted to know exactly where they were taking him, what the floor looked like, the level of commitment of the staff, whether Jonathan would be comfortable, if a doctor would be there to help him. To me, the hospital seemed dark and barren, isolated, with only a skeleton crew who resented being there on a Saturday night.

He was my older son. That night I thought he would never take heroin again. This was not the Jonathan I knew, the one Linda and I had raised, the one organizing workers in the streets of Albany, speaking eloquently about the ideals of social justice, challenging the imaginative possibilities of life. No, this was not the boy who at nine years old had made "Got the Blues" his father's favorite tune because his father so much enjoyed listening to him play it on the Steinway piano in our living room. Nor was this the young man turning 21, the son to whom a father had written a birthday letter on that day, as he always did on each birthday.

> ...One day you will be a father looking at your son with the joy that only fathers know. Perhaps you will play "Got the Blues" on the piano for him. I know you will read him books. I will think then as I do now that I am fortunate to have such a wonderful man for a son...

I said good-bye to Jonathan, hugged him, watched him walk down the dark corridor through some swinging doors to the elevator that would take him upstairs. I felt a terrible sense of separation and loneliness as he walked away and disappeared into that night.

Jonathan would never see the inside of our home again. Yes, I wish I had taken him home to Dartmouth that night. But the horror of withdrawal had stunned me like the sudden shriek of an unseen raven; it was too overwhelming, too frightening to imagine. And the idea of bringing him home made no rational sense. No doubt he would have been back on the streets looking for heroin in a few days if we had taken him home.

Yes, of course, I wish there was some way I could have stayed on top of him, never let him out of my sight, as Carroll O'Connor suggests on those television ads he made after his son died. Yes, of course, I wish I had wrestled him down to the ground, pinning those demons to the mat until they gave up. Of course, I do.

> Missing me one place search another,
> I stop somewhere waiting for you.

～

Everyone warned us Jonathan had a tough battle ahead. "Heroin addiction kills most people," a local psychologist told us in his office one night that week. "Only a few survive. Around 75 percent relapse in the first year."

But Jonathan had a better chance than most, everyone seemed to agree. He was well-educated, came from a solid family, had a lot of love and support to draw on. All that provided a cushion of hope. He should be able to make it through, they claimed.

Despite these reassurances, from the day Jonathan entered Butler I lived with the continuous terror that he was going to die. Whenever the phone rang, my stomach churned. Wrong numbers in the middle of the night triggered cold sweat. I grew to hate the random calls from phone marketeers. I distrusted the medical doctors and the well-meaning drug counselors. I could not fully embrace the 12-step methods or the support groups.

I kept myself busy, though. I had recently been appointed Dean of Continuing Education by the new chancellor, moving from Chairman of the English Department to this hard-core administrative position. It was strikingly different from what I had been doing for most of the past 20 years, teaching and writing as a professor. I saw this new role as a challenge, an exciting opportunity to expand public education throughout the region. The chancellor shared that vision and energy.

We began to open new off-campus sites throughout the Southcoast, hoping to expand the dream in the name of the university. We moved into new buildings, created new catalogs, made television and radio ads celebrating the importance of lifelong learning.

I came into my office every morning, greeted my staff, smiled, worked relentlessly, head down, developing innovative programs for adult learners. I was in my car, driving endlessly to our new sites, back and forth, trying to fulfill a promise; then in my office again helping to pioneer some of the first cyber-ed programs offered anywhere in the country, always looking to the horizon.

Yes, I was engaged, exhilarated, as if on a roller coaster, but it was always Jonathan I was thinking of, always the image of Jonathan healthy and smiling, and then the image of Jonathan disappearing. It was as if I were on stage in an auditorium and only Jonathan was there sitting among all the empty seats; then all the seats were filled except for the one Jonathan had been in, now empty and silent.

AA Books, Telephones
and the Health Community

*F*or me, the journey to Butler that stifling summer evening was the beginning of a long grieving process that will never completely end. Despite the clichés of good intention from counselors and reporters, there is no such thing as "closure" for this kind of loss. Nor are there distinct stages to pass through and overcome. Distance created by time may help, but even then time and distance can collapse in a moment as the image of the beloved returns unexpectedly and the heart opens to embrace the vanishing ghost.

When Linda, Jeremy, and I went to visit Jonathan the next morning at Butler, he was resting quietly on his hospital bed after a merciful night that turned out to produce a very mild withdrawal. It was the first time we had been on a detox floor. Several patients were veterans of the place, though; they had AA books, the Big Book, Bibles on their shelves. Some seemed at home here, moving about, chatting with each other. Many had nowhere to go once they left Butler except back out on the streets, and this accounted in part for their frequent relapses.

We were all surprised Jonathan's withdrawal had been so mild. He hadn't suffered the flu-like pain, the terrifying cramps and shaking, the profuse sweating that typifies this kind of sickness. He had been given some drugs to alleviate the symptoms and they may have helped him, along with his own forced reduction of heroin use the previous few days in New York when he lacked ready cash.

I was thinking yesterday about seeing Jonathan at Butler detox the first day he was brought there. How sad he was. We walked into his room where he sat on a bed crying. He wanted us to know it was not our fault, that he had had a good childhood, with loving parents and brother, that nothing terrible had happened

to him and that he loved us. How could that be? I wondered. Here
was my son, in a setting I had only seen in movies, telling us we
had not done something terrible to him. We must have! Why else
would he be here? I knew so little about addiction and what would
take place in the days and months to come.

I noticed a pay phone against the wall in the lounge area in continuous use that day, a channel to drug dealers who would arrange drop-offs
for their customers (I later discovered). In fact, telephones were very
much a part of the drug culture we were getting to know. The phone
was the one inanimate object—except for heroin itself—that seemed
to take on its own life. Like heroin, it looms up as a haunting image
threaded throughout these memories.

The pay phones on the streets of New York, the ones scattered
along the road into Providence, the ones at Butler and at other hospitals—Miriam, Roosevelt—the ones at Hazelden in Minnesota and at
the Fellowship Club in New York, the ones in halfway houses outside
of Palm Springs and in San Francisco, and the gigantic phone bills on
Jonathan's credit cards long before he entered the hospital—all these
run together in memory; and the phones in our own home ringing
with calls from around the country from people we had consulted
for advice, phones carrying dreadful messages of wrong numbers late
at night making our hearts sink with the weight of fear, phones with
unrecognized voices that jump-start new levels of anxiety, only to be
quelled when those voices are identified as part of the common call
of the salesperson—yes, all these phones tie together the wires of a
changed life.

Like the call coming in the middle of the night from Jonathan when
he was still a graduate student at Amherst—the phone ringing out of
nowhere in the darkness, Jonathan's voice terrified on the other end of
the line; it was about his roommate.

"Scott's dead," he said trembling as I listened to him on the phone
next to our bed.

"His father just called. He died in a scuba diving accident on vacation in Mexico."

Jonathan was alone in an empty house that dark night. He needed to make a family connection.

We know now that Scott had been taking heroin; he may have started Jonathan on it. Scott's death shook Jonathan, disturbed him for a long time. It couldn't shake him from his addiction, though.

We wanted Jonathan to return to us.

But is it possible Jonathan wanted something else? The sociologist Jack Katz once wrote: "To be cool is to view the immediate social situation as ontologically inferior, non-transcendent, and too mundane to compel one's complete attentions. A common way of being cool is to realize or affect a moderate drug mood: the 'cool cat' of black street life has its origins in the culture of the heroin world."

Had the situation become too mundane for him? Had the culture itself become too ordinary, too superficial, too meaningless? Had Jonathan become one of the "angelheaded hipsters" the poet Allen Ginsberg had described, "burning for the heavenly connection to the starry dynamo in the machinery of night"?

Yes, I wish I could speak to Jonathan about all this.

~

While Jonathan was at Butler, we began our own phone crusade, trying to make certain he got the best care possible and trying to assure a smooth transition for him to move directly from detox in Butler to an inpatient treatment facility. It was as if we believed the stronger the network the greater the chance Jonathan had for survival. I began to read voraciously about heroin addiction, its physiology and psychology, its treatments and its possibilities for recovery. Books about drugs were stacked in piles throughout our house. We were concerned about Jonathan, of course, but also about Jeremy, his only brother, and about ourselves. Heroin addiction clearly affected our entire family.

We talked endlessly to Dr. Fine in New York, to experts in Massachusetts, to local therapists and drug counselors, to family and friends. And we launched an excruciating battle with Greensprings, the business agent for Western Pennsylvania Blue Cross Blue Shield, the insurance company Jonathan was associated with through his union work. Greensprings was considered by many as the worst agent in the country for those pursuing care for drug addiction, we quickly learned. The very name "Greensprings" sent waves of revulsion through the entire recovery community.

NYC and Miriam

While Jonathan struggled at Butler, I decided to drive back down to New York to pick up his clothes and other belongings left in his union associate's apartment in Queens. I was exhausted and Linda and others advised against making such a trip—a one-day roundtrip at that—but I felt compelled to go, to clean up the New York business as much as possible. I wanted to feel I was doing something.

In the apartment, I took the pressed shirts on hangers out of his closet. They appeared upright, at attention. Then I opened his dresser drawers and noticed how perfectly neat his towels and underwear were laid out.

"They remind me of the papers, so well organized, in the box I took home from Jonathan's union office a few days ago," I told my friend Jim Nee, who had driven with me to New York that day. "Look how well organized they are. How neat. He must get this from Linda." Every piece of clothing in the dresser seemed exactly right, folded smartly, in perfect place.

There was a silence in that neatness, though, as if I had come to clean out the room of a dead man. These material goods, their texture soft and gentle to my touch, gave evidence of a life that had resisted chaos but had finally been defeated. It was as if Jonathan had disappeared, leaving only external traces of himself.

On the same day I traveled to New York, Jonathan was diagnosed with a severe blood infection and immediately transferred from Butler to Miriam, a medical hospital in Providence that turned out to be ill prepared to treat the complexities of drug addiction. Jonathan was irritable and jumpy, no match for the medical staff.

I remember how volatile he was in the hospital a few days later. He had a life-threatening infection from the use of needles, and we were told it could infect his heart and kill him at any time. Jonathan wanted to leave the hospital—crazed from the lack of heroin. I was so afraid; I could not seem to reach him. One night, while he was being especially difficult, insisting he would sign himself out the next day, I stood over his bed and wept. "Please Jonathan," I begged, "Stay here and let us find the best help for you. If you refuse, I'm so afraid that you will die—I WILL NOT LET YOU DIE. I am your mother and I love you so much but I can't bear to watch you do this to my child."

As he always did, Jonathan listened quietly. Even as a teenager, he was usually very reasonable and listened to our advice. Of course, as we now knew, he did not always follow that advice. Jonathan lay in bed and watched me sob, tears rolling down his beautiful round face. He could not bear my pain, but his was worse.

~

Within a day or two at Miriam, Jonathan made the acquaintance of another patient, thin and pale, a prostitute who had just had the veins in her arm removed because they had become so polluted. She had a friend, a man wearing a religious collar who came to visit her regularly, pretending spiritual counsel, insisting to the hospital staff that he could take her home when she was ready. "He's evil, Dad," Jonathan told me. But the prostitute and her man smuggled heroin into the hospital, the connection with the outside world apparently made through the small chapel on the ground floor. Jonathan mixed the heroin with the intravenous medication pumping into his veins.

Later we noticed that whenever a hospital cart would roll by with drugs or needles Jonathan would focus on it, drawn by instinct to the supply. "Did you see that?" I asked Linda. "It's like a magnet drawing him in." We couldn't believe Jonathan was taking heroin in the hospital. It seemed as if he were drifting into madness.

I can only imagine what he thought of the orthodox rabbi who came to visit him, asking him to wrap his left arm with the tefillin, invoking the power in that ritual to counter the power of the heroin entering the same arm.

After painstaking research, we decided to send Jonathan to Hazelden, a place first mentioned by the psychologist and counselor, Larry Barnett. Hazelden is located in Center City, Minnesota, about an hour north of the twin cities of Minneapolis and St. Paul, a well-respected national center for substance abuse treatment with 28-day inpatient programs and a network of after-care facilities throughout the country.

We wanted to be certain Jonathan's transition to Center City went as smoothly as possible when his infection improved and he was out of immediate danger, but the matter of insurance became an ugly problem once more. Greensprings did not really believe in inpatient care and refused at first to cover Jonathan's recovery there.

"Yes, we're well aware of Greensprings," Hazelden informed us. "We've never once been able to get them to pay for inpatient treatment here."

From Hazelden's perspective, Greensprings reflected the worst elements of health-care reform, ultimately leading to the shut-down of needed facilities. As Dr. Fine put it, "More and more people suffering from addiction will have to die on the streets before the country wakes up to the horror of agents like Greensprings." Fewer and fewer people could afford the kind of care Jonathan needed. Even Hazelden, a well-subsidized institution with a substantial endowment, cost $9600 for the 28-day program. How many people could afford that without the help of health insurance? And how many people cared?

We finally assured Hazelden we would pay if the insurance company didn't, but we kept up the pressure on Greensprings, asking Dr. Fine and Larry Barnett in New York to intervene on our behalf. We also asked Senator Kennedy's Office in Massachusetts for help and talked with Deb Beck in Pennsylvania, a well-known advocate for the recovery community, who phoned the Pennsylvania Commissioner of Health to argue our case. In the end, Greensprings yielded. It was the powerful voice of politics, not the studied voice of medicine, that won the day for us.

As the staff at Hazelden acknowledged, we had won one of the very few victories of this kind over an unsavory enemy. But it is not the kind of victory one really cares about. There is no sense of triumph, no adrenaline rush attached to the win. I look back at it now and remain saddened by it. The energy expended. The resources called up. The networks established. I am ashamed we live in a country where such things happen so often. It is unfair to ask ordinary people in crisis to do this. Unfortunately we do, all the time. That's what makes agencies like Greensprings so powerful and so arrogant.

In the Air to Hazelden

*A*fter ten days at Miriam Hospital, Jonathan was ready to leave for Hazelden. But I was not ready to see him go.

The doctors had done a good job getting his blood infection under control, but they were frustrated. "We don't really know how to handle a patient like Jonathan," they explained. "We're not trained to deal with heroin addicts." They were sympathetic, but clearly content to see him on his way.

Driving with Jonathan from Miriam to Boston for his flight to Hazelden, we listened to the news on the radio, reports humming with violence and trouble, and I thought about the brutality my father had known living as a little boy in Czarist Russia, the arrogance and misfortune easily recognizable in the faceless world that seemed to surround Jonathan now. I wanted Jonathan to be safe.

"I'm considering flying out with him," I had told the staff at Hazelden.

"That's really unnecessary," they responded. Foolish, they seemed to suggest.

Like Butler, Hazelden had strict rules about visiting. "Yes, you could stay overnight on the grounds once you arrive, but as soon as Jonathan is settled in his own room, you won't be able to see him again," they said.

In the end, I listened to them. I didn't go.

Instead, I watched Jonathan's plane rise in the sky above Logan that day, mesmerized by its spell. It moved slowly like a silver bullet floating across the puffy clouds, lonely in the heavens, quietly disappearing into the blue firmament. My eyes seemed fixed on it. When it became invisible, I held to the empty space just as I would a year later at Jonathan's grave the day we buried him.

When Jonathan arrived that night at Hazelden, he immediately called to let us know he was there, safe and secure. They put him in a room with several other men, and he began the program, quickly adjusting to the official routine. Soon he had his own room. Jonathan always got his own room eventually, a reward for doing well, he claimed. People liked him, even in these institutional facilities. "He makes us laugh," they would say. "He cares." I could hear his laughter welling up from deep within his body when they said that, resonant and spontaneous, exploding into the world.

Yet he was detached, separate from the rest, isolated and lonely. Heroin marked him out, even there. And it was just that, I suppose, that sense of being unique, special, that destroyed him. Nobody could tell him anything he didn't already know. He came to believe through his heroin deceptions he could outwit everyone. He was never arrogant, always gentle, often compassionate throughout this last year. But he really didn't fit in. He thought I was too abstract, too intellectually removed, he once claimed. Later, he told me he thought reading was similar to taking drugs. Looking through the library one day after he died, I discovered an intriguing book that suggested how addictive reading could be.

~

On Rosh Hashana, the Jewish New Year, I flew out to Hazelden with Linda and Jeremy for a scheduled family program. We were together, resolute despite the rubble.

Linda, the mother, Tufts graduate, high school math teacher, secure with lists and numbers. She was fearful now, anxious she might say the wrong thing to her baby boy. She wished so much she could shake him out of this funk, tell him to "cut the crap," as she liked to put it, cut the crap, return to me.

Jeremy, the younger brother, Tufts undergraduate, deeply devoted and loyal to Jonathan. For him, Jonathan would always be the best friend, the older brother who baby–sat for him, taught him to ride a bicycle on the concrete playground in the back of our large apartment complex in New Bedford, endured his playful wrestling, brought him to college parties with real girls.

And me, the father, the professor, wondering, like the others, how our family and the world had been turned upside down and inside out.

I have a picture of Jonathan and Jeremy sitting close to each other on our couch early one morning in Walla Walla. It's 1974. Jeremy, barely three months old, nestled in the arms of his big brother, the five-year-old. They are both in their cotton pajamas, gazing out the front window of our little rented ranch house with the asparagus garden in the backyard. The two brothers are riveted as they watch Linda slowly drive from the house down the street, taking me in our tan Plymouth Fury the few blocks to the college campus for my morning classes. Two young boys, pressing their sweet round faces to the glass, anxious and proud, soulmates alone for the first time. They sit together, not moving, waiting patiently for the return of their loving mother. It is not a photograph, but a picture that haunts me now wherever I go.

So we went to Hazelden as a family, rooted and determined, despite the whirlwind.

Hazelden is a large pastoral retreat, quiet and peaceful, stretching over many acres with buildings connected by an intricate network of corridors. It has a gym, an auditorium, eating areas, break-out rooms for meetings and discussions, a small detox hospital with medical staff, and an area for administrative personnel. We could only visit with Jonathan for short periods. The family program was an opportunity designed for us, an exploration of our complicity and co-dependency with the addict. We joined other families—mainly affluent middle class—exchanged ideas, went through therapeutic group sessions, and generally felt a sense of relief by recognizing others like ourselves experiencing similar pain.

Except for the assigned times, we were not allowed to see Jonathan, the rationale being that we were better off wrestling with our problems together with others in difficulty. On a few occasions, though, Jeremy went over to see Jonathan in his dormitory, sitting in the Day Room with him, watching television together on the soft couch, separate from the rest of the family. Jeremy was worried about Jonathan, as we all were, particularly frightened about what would happen when he left Hazelden at the end of the 28 days. He couldn't figure out exactly what to say, but he was glad to be there with his brother, sitting together, side by side.

None of us knew exactly what to do. I walked through the woods one day with a Harvard historian, recently divorced, who had just arrived to see his son and participate in the family program.

"I don't know what to do," he said. "Any ideas?"

I knew, like me, he wanted to know. I comforted him the best I could, trying to explain to him what I had been experiencing the last few days, what I had learned. Our talking to each other was valuable no doubt. But I had very little to tell him.

"We'll have to stay in touch back in Massachusetts," he offered as we approached the end of the path.

"Yes," I agreed.

We never did.

～

We met Vicki, Jonathan's senior counselor, a former drug addict, in her early 30s, fragile and proud. She had been working at Hazelden for a few months, anxious in her devotion to serve, still trying to pull herself together. I admired her tenacity.

At a family meeting near the end of our stay, she announced to us with some sense of victory: "Jonathan has agreed to go to our Fellowship Club in New York City." It was a victory, she explained, because during most of his stay at Hazelden Jonathan had resisted the prospect of further treatment. She seemed pleased and satisfied. When I heard all this, though, I wanted to take her neck in my bare hands and strangle her. For me, New York represented the ultimate risk. How could they dare send Jonathan back into the streets and neighborhoods he knew so well? Why hadn't they at least arranged for a space in the halfway house Hazelden owned in St. Paul? Didn't this well-known institution know what it was doing?

I realize now it wouldn't have mattered. A couple of blocks away from the house in St. Paul was a crack hangout. Jonathan could have scored drugs there anytime.

Fear dominated the entire year we all struggled for Jonathan's recovery. I was afraid to say the wrong thing, afraid I might make him go take more drugs. Maybe if I had been firmer and said "cut the crap"—maybe if we had left him alone—maybe...who will ever know?

∽

Jonathan was reading the novel *Forrest Gump* while we were at Hazelden. I walked by his room on the ground floor one night, saw him alone at the window, asked him about the book. "It's a good book," he said. "I'm really enjoying it."

We talked through the glass for a few minutes. Jonathan, separate and alone, holding a book; his father outside, alone, looking in through the glass, wondering what his son is thinking.

He would often tell me about a book he was reading.

"There's a book by a French writer about the power of stories," he once said, a slim volume that had just caught his attention. "It makes me think about those stories you created sitting on my bed before I went to sleep at night."

He would fall asleep to those stories when he was a little boy, and I would return to his room later to check on him, to be sure he was safe. Cowboy Jonathan would always be sleeping with his eyes shut gently like an angel after a long day.

∽

In his room at Hazelden the next day, we sat on his bed, trying to talk to each other about important matters, but we never quite got there. After a while, he took out a paper with a written exercise he had been given in his group. It was xeroxed with short statements designed to help two people share feelings. He went down the list on the paper, responding by talking about what bothered him about himself. Jonathan was a big man, overweight then, a lot of that weight gained over the last few years. "It disturbs me," he said. "I know it's something I should focus on." As it turned out, he never would.

We tried to do the exercise together, joking at times from what must have been mutual discomfort and embarrassment. I am not sure if he suggested the exercise out of an assigned obligation or because he genuinely believed we could both find something in it. I felt I was not offering enough, although I wanted to. It was, after all, only an exercise.

By the time Jonathan was ready to leave Hazelden, he had heard enough about exercises. I had too. Jonathan knew what needed to be done. The rest was up to him.

The other places on his long and lonely journey—the halfway houses, the groups, the detox centers—would give him some margin of safety and some sense of rules and structures, some fellowship as well, but they would make little difference to him. He needed to connect with something deep within him, some essential self, if he could find it and if it were there. He needed a conversion to turn his life around. Perhaps if he had created a different image of himself, if he had a respectable white-collar job, a slim body, suave clothes—perhaps then he would have made it through this brutal and arrogant world. But his inability or unwillingness to create this image can only be marked as a symptom of the problem. It wasn't the cause.

Return to the Big Apple

When Jonathan left Minnesota and flew back East to New York, Linda and I picked him up at La Guardia and brought him to the Hazelden Fellowship Club near Gramercy Park, a well-established neighborhood with tree-lined streets in Manhattan. We met with Don Hewett, the director, and walked through the old house, hoping that Jonathan would quickly assimilate and find a meaningful job. The Fellowship Club was about as much like the Hazelden campus as New York City is like Minnesota. Here we were close to the rhythm of the city streets, ethnic diversity, working-class life. I was convinced it was the most dangerous place in the world for Jonathan, especially with his intimate knowledge of these streets.

Jonathan's senior counselor in the house was Paul Campbell, a reformed drug addict, who had frightened and alienated his wealthy family during his addiction and who now wanted to do whatever he could to help others with similar problems. Jonathan also began to see Dr. Fine again to map out a way to develop skills he had lost through drugs, skills to help him socialize and regain the sense of community.

Drugs can thwart emotional growth, arrest development, and the doctors claimed that given the long period of time Jonathan had probably used drugs, stretching back to smoking pot in high school, some of his basic emotional patterns had most likely not matured. In some areas, he was simply a young boy who needed to go through a typical learning curve before he reached manhood.

He seemed to be settling in. But not for long.

~

Jonathan's first relapse came about two weeks after he entered the house in New York. The call came directly to my office at the university, the first of several, immediately snapping me out of the routine of a dean's work, the illusion of bureaucratic safety within the walls of an academic institution.

Jonathan had found heroin again on the hectic streets of New York, and under the rules of the house he was obligated to leave immediately. Since it was late in the afternoon, though, and the streets seethed with seduction for heroin addicts, the counselors agreed Jonathan could stay overnight, providing I picked him up in the morning. I was in a panic, went home, told Linda what had happened, tried to be rational and strong in the face of her own devastation at the news.

Jonathan wouldn't agree to come home, I thought, but I suggested to Linda that might be the best idea if I could somehow convince him.

"Bringing him home will only lead to disaster," she insisted as she prepared supper in the kitchen for the two of us. "He needs professional help. Something we can't give him. If you do bring him back, I'll have to leave the house."

There was little reason to pursue such discussion anyway, since I would have to wait to see how Jonathan reacted when I got to New York. So I dropped it.

Early the next morning, I drove over that familiar highway again, the one that winds across Rhode Island and Connecticut to New York, noticing the phone booths and the Burger Kings along the way. I could hear the murmur of the city when I finally sat down with Jonathan, Hewett, and Campbell in a cramped office upstairs in the halfway house, ready to discuss a strategy for Jonathan's future.

"You don't know how terrified I am," I told Jonathan in that crowded room, trying to understand his pain, working hard to uncover a way to help him. "I'm worried you're going to die."

I took a small piece of paper from a pad on Hewett's desk and wrote my name and phone numbers on it with a note at the top: "In case of death call..." Jonathan looked at the paper as I handed it to him, and then, with a nod of understanding, silently folded it and placed it carefully in his wallet.

We all agreed if Jonathan stayed clean, he could return to the Fellowship Club in two weeks. In the meantime, he needed to find housing in New York and continue to look for work. Hewett suggested the YMCA in the Chelsea area, not too far from where we were.

"Please come home," I urged him as we got back out in the street.

"No way," he replied. "I want to stay in New York and work on the program," he claimed with a sincerity hard to deny.

Before we took the room at the Y, Jonathan wanted to check out another place he'd heard about. It was a horror, a broken-down flophouse on the edge of the Village, near 12th Avenue. We walked by a man, perhaps in his 50s, urinating on the side of the building when we entered. The clerk, leaning on the scarred wooden desk, seemed to be wondering what we were doing there. It was a place for addicts and prostitutes, down-and-outers. The clerk's face was vacant of interest, perhaps wondering if we were the subjects of a bad joke, but he brought us upstairs, to a room no bigger than a closet, along a long empty corridor.

The whole place seemed as if it had been abandoned, quiet and in shambles like a dilapidated amusement park. The floors were warped and slanted, and I began to feel nauseated. I was sure we had entered a twilight zone. I looked at Jonathan and should have realized how much trouble he was in. In the old days, we would have laughed and joked about this worn-out funhouse with crazy floors and mirrors, but I couldn't find even a tired smile on his face now. Jonathan seemed deadly serious, willing to stay.

He must have wanted to get rid of me, the sooner the better. Where he stayed made little difference to him. What he needed was money and heroin, another encounter with the needle, with what Tav Sparks, an addict turned therapist, referred to as the perverse embodiment of the gladiator, the knight, the sorcerer. Yes, what I should have done was thrown him in the car, chained him to the seat, taken him howling home.

He did agree to stay at the Y, though, and so I got a room for him there, a narrow space with a bed and barren desk. Two people could hardly move in it, but Jonathan seemed satisfied.

"You should try to get a job while you're here," I reminded him. "And take advantage of the gym. You could lose some weight."

Although I paid for his room, I refused to give him any additional money, fearing he would use it for drugs. It was a useless strategy. I discovered later he would spend his days out on the street panhandling. But he must have worked on his recovery. He made it back into the house at the end of the two-week period.

When we said goodbye in front of the YMCA early that evening, I saw tears well up in his eyes. I walked across the street to my car, not turning around, not wanting him to see my own tears. As I drove away, I looked back, but he had disappeared, vanished into the misery of that small room in the Y that had become his solitary refuge.

Thanksgiving and the New Year

We hoped Jonathan would now seriously begin to work on regaining his old self, return to his real identity, be that normal young man we used to know. And after he went back to the Fellowship Club, he seemed to make progress for the next three months, until the end of December when he was almost ready to be discharged.

Linda, Jeremy, and I visited Jonathan over Thanksgiving, eating a holiday meal with him at Man Ray's restaurant in Chelsea. Like the Jewish holiday of Passover, Thanksgiving had always been an important time for our family, a time for ritual around the table, a time for memory and good cheer, a reminder of the bounty of life despite the hard times of history. But these meetings with Jonathan were growing difficult for me, in part because I had seen close up the squalor Jonathan was willing to live in, in part because I wanted him to spring free, leave this prison of addiction, live a reasonable life above ground. I was having trouble that Thanksgiving joining the light banter around the table in that stylish restaurant. The clichés of recovery irked me; the calm at the surface threatened to break apart. I know this annoyed the others, and I am sorry for that, just as I am sorry I didn't simply take my son by the collar that day and drag him home.

Sitting around that family table in Chelsea, listening to Jonathan talk about his program for recovery and the daily matters of the Fellowship Club, I wanted to believe he was done with heroin, cured. Sure, he might drink a few beers, I thought, smoke some pot, but he had conquered heroin. It was an experience he had gone through, endured, and he was now emerging on the other side of it. Few others had taken such a journey, my Romantic imagination insisted.

Toward the end of December, Jonathan began to make plans to leave the halfway house and get his own place in Manhattan. He was anxious and confused, not at all clear where he was going to stay, whom he was going to live with, or how he could afford to support himself. We again agreed to help pay his rent, but we all felt he needed to develop a blueprint to give him appropriate boundaries and reasonable goals, to make him feel comfortable and conventional.

~

Linda gave me a wonderful party that same winter month, a brunch for my 50th birthday. It was a complete surprise when I walked into the restaurant that day, and I was so pleased that Linda, knotted with her own anguish, had the strength to do that for me. It felt good to look into the grinning faces of my friends and family, gathered together in the intimacy of that restaurant near the ocean that Sunday morning, friends and family clapping and cheering, wishing me well, as the waves battered the ice-covered rocks along the coastline. It was refreshing. But later, when I got up at the table to make a few brief remarks, to thank everyone for coming, for the gifts, for the poetry, for the kind words and warm wishes, I looked out and suddenly felt the weight of Jonathan's absence. He was the only one missing.

There was a pause in the rhythm of my talk that day, a moment when I was ready to give up, sit down in defeat. I worked through it though, looking at my aging father, nearly 90 then, sitting near me. "…And I can only hope I have his genes," I concluded.

But without Jonathan's laughter in the room, his beaming smile, there was something incomplete, a beat forever lost in the cadence of that magical moment.

~

On New Year's Eve, Linda and I drove to Boston to celebrate First Night. We ate a rich Italian dinner in the North End, veal and pasta with a creamy cheese sauce, drank a couple of glasses of fine wine, and then walked around the downtown area, bustling with party-goers fighting the freezing weather. There were thousands of people crowding the streets that night, ice sculptors with spotlights catching the moon glow, singers and noise makers, clowns, all greeting the new year. We were exhausted when we climbed into bed.

Early the next morning, the phone rang in our hotel room. It was Paul Campbell.

"I'm sorry to have to call you with bad news, especially on New Year's Day," Campbell began. "I called you at home, and Jeremy said you were up there in Boston. I'm very sorry. But Jonathan has relapsed again."

They had no choice, Campbell explained with sorrow in his voice. They were now forced to expel Jonathan from the Fellowship Club, outdoors, permanently.

Unlike his first relapse, this time Jonathan didn't want to talk with me on the phone. And he refused to stay in the house until I got there, causing alarm among the Fellowship staff that he might be out on the streets taking heroin before I arrived. When I did get to New York, it was mid-afternoon, a holiday, and as I had no clear idea what was best to do next—although I realized we had to do something—keep moving. Jonathan was waiting across the street from the Fellowship Club, sitting by himself on a bench in the small neighborhood park reading *The New York Times*.

When we got back in the house, Campbell and I, along with Don Hewett, reviewed the options with him. "Don't forget the deal, Jonathan. You promised if you relapsed again you'd enter another 28-day inpatient program."

But he didn't want to go back to Hazelden, and when Campbell checked Hazelden by phone, he discovered there was a waiting list anyway.

Jonathan was restless and, in retrospect, clearly in the midst of drug withdrawal, aggravating and aggravated, unable to make clear and rational decisions and choices. He resisted any idea about another treatment center, and so we began to look for a bed for him in a ten-day detox center right in New York City. It was particularly difficult because it was a holiday and a weekend.

We called Roosevelt Hospital. They claimed they had an available bed, but it was too late to admit him, so we would have to wait until the next day. They seemed to want to get home for the holiday, avoid the paperwork, shove off.

Running out of options, Hewett and Campbell finally decided to call an addiction center they did not know firsthand but had seen advertised on local television. "We're suspicious," they said, "but it's about all we've got left."

~

It was dark when I left the halfway house with Jonathan carrying a few of his basic belongings to the car. We headed uptown to the West Side to check him in to this place known only through its commercials on the flickering TV screens of New York. I was frightened, not at all certain Jonathan would be taken care of there. I am not sure what Jonathan was thinking, although I assumed he felt a mixture of shame and rage, anger at himself and at the world.

The late-middle-aged man who answered the doorbell at the detox center looked to me like an alcoholic or addict: unshaven, slovenly, a smoker. "What kind of insurance do you have?" he demanded immediately. When I asked questions about the facility, he quickly reminded me there was probably no other place in New York City on New Year's night that would accept Jonathan, especially since it was too late to validate the insurance with any company.

"We'll give him a small dose of methadone to help with the withdrawal and then we'll slowly wean him off of it," he explained as he lit another cigarette. "During the next week or so, Jonathan will begin to clean his body of the toxins circulating through his system."

Jonathan appeared frightened, and I was skeptical. "Can I at least see the inpatient facilities?" I asked, looking at the ashtray on his desk filled with dead butts. "Can I make sure they're okay?"

"No, that's impossible," I was quickly told. "A violation of the rules. Unfair to the other patients on the floor already in treatment."

Realizing I was not going to be able to change these rules and procedures, I finally retreated, retrieved Jonathan's duffel bag from the car, handed it to him in the doorway, and watched him once again vanish into a dark netherworld.

Although I wasn't allowed to visit Jonathan for any significant length of time, I decided to stay in New York until I felt he was settled. I called Dr. Fine to let him know what had happened. "I don't feel comfortable with the place," I told him.

"Try moving Jonathan to the detox ward at Roosevelt Hospital," he suggested. "I can see him there on a regular basis." Fine was unfamiliar with the other place, but thought my impressions of its nightmare setting were most likely accurate.

Needing to gain some focus on what seemed like chaos and confusion, I went by the Fellowship Club the next morning to talk again with Paul Campbell. "I've got to do something with Jonathan," I told him as I paced back and forth in his office. "I don't like the place he's in at all."

"Let him stay where he is," Campbell advised. "It's the best thing for him. You should head home. Back to Massachusetts. You need some rest anyway. And there's really nothing more you can do right now."

But Jonathan called the Fellowship Club while I was with Campbell and asked that I come and get him immediately. The place was terrible, he said, a hellhole filled with street people and court-designated patients, a twilight zone of dereliction where no one even came by his bed in the darkness to check on him. Jonathan's report confirmed all my fears, of course, and I was ready in an instant to pluck him out of this flea-bag excuse for a drug addiction center. Ironically, it turned out that Greensprings, our anchor in the swirling world of health insurance, would pay this self-promoting center for Jonathan's one-night treatment without contacting us at all.

Campbell was worried that I planned to take care of Jonathan at home, an idea that he, like Linda, opposed and thought foolish. I explained to him that my plans were less ambitious. I only wanted to get Jonathan into Roosevelt. I planned to take him to the emergency room, the best bet for admission.

Roosevelt Hospital and Heroin Addiction

When I arrived at the detox center, Jonathan was standing outside waiting patiently on the doorstep with his clothes carefully folded into the duffel bag beside him. As he got in the car, I told him we were going over to Roosevelt, a few blocks away. He didn't seem to be suffering from withdrawal, had made it through the night without any physical problems, and didn't appear in need of much help. He told me as much, clearly not happy to be going to another institution.

"I don't need detox, Dad," he explained to me. "I feel fine."

But the streets hummed with those typical undercurrents of chaotic misfortune, and his mind was certainly not clear for rational calculation. We headed to Roosevelt despite Jonathan's insistence that it was unnecessary.

"I'll never go to another program when I get out of here," he claimed as we entered the hospital together.

I sat quietly next to Jonathan on the hard metal chairs in the outer admissions area off the main foyer at Roosevelt Hospital that day. Eventually a woman at the desk called his name and he went up to talk with her for a few minutes. When he returned he seemed resigned to his fate, at least for the next week or so.

"She wants me to use the phone on the wall over there," he said pointing. I watched him as he dialed the extension for the addiction floor, giving information over that phone, answering a series of questions, searching through his wallet for the appropriate cards, being told to wait until they could check his insurance. They would be downstairs to see him in a while, they said.

We sat there, father and son, for a long time until someone finally came and brought us to another office where we sat and waited again. Did Jonathan really have to go through this? I wondered. The process of these institutions was growing increasingly typical, clichéd, stale, annoying.

A young woman, also waiting to be admitted, sat next to us. She was a frequent patient at Roosevelt, accustomed to the routine and long hours. She seemed calm, content. People make a habit of coming into detox units, I thought, leaving and then returning, a dull round of motion, endless in its pursuit of itself. Very much like the bureaucracy. I could only pray that Jonathan would not get caught on that pinwheel of false desire.

It turned out the rules at Roosevelt were stricter than those at Butler. Officially, I was told, Jonathan could have no visitors during the week he was in the detox unit, although I could talk with him on the phone. When the staff came in their white uniforms to take Jonathan from the admissions area, I could only stand there, as I had done so many times before, and watch him walk away, disappearing into the elevator, lifting him to an upstairs floor, locked and out of sight.

I decided to remain in New York for at least one more day to see if there was anything else I could do for Jonathan, and myself. I wanted to make sure Dr. Fine visited him and, despite the rules and regulations, I was determined to visit him as well.

Early the following morning I made a series of phone calls to Dr. Fine, to arrange for him to see Jonathan, and to the chief physician on Jonathan's floor, to convince him that as Jonathan's father I had every right to see my son. The chief had a response for me, of course, an argument based on an established foundation of bureaucratic equity and fairness: Since other patients were not allowed to have visitors, it would be perceived as special treatment for Jonathan if I came to visit. I knew the shape and contour of the argument. I am sure I had used it myself many times. I didn't let up, though.

Don't you think a father should be able to see his son? How many fathers have requested to see their sons in Roosevelt? Who could help a son more than a father? What kind of hospital are you running anyway?

Eventually the chief physician yielded to the dean's barrage. I could come to the detox unit, but I needed to melt into the scene, act as if I were one of Dr. Fine's associates rather than Jonathan's father, pretend

I was someone other than myself. When Fine heard about the plan, he was rattled at first but then expressed genuine admiration for my apparent skill in convincing the hospital that I should see my son.

"You must be an excellent administrator," he said warmly over the phone.

We agreed to meet with Jonathan that afternoon.

~

Although I had often spoken with Dr. Fine over the past several months, I had never met him in person. He was the director of one of the toughest addiction units in the Bronx, and I expected, I suppose, to see that toughness reflected in his look. So I was surprised by his appearance when I first spotted him in the lobby at Roosevelt. He wore an earring, open collar, tan shirt with a jacket. Was he gay? I wondered. He was clearly Jewish, with short hair, trim build, about five-eleven. Here was the physician I had heard so much about.

We rode up the automatic elevator in which I had last seen Jonathan disappear, pressed the button to buzz through the locked door guarding the corridor of the detox unit, and entered as the metal door clanked shut behind us. Dr. Fine played the role, introducing me as Dr. Waxler, which he would later point out was not a lie, and then we were taken by Jonathan's nurse to see him in a room down the tiled hallway. "Oh, yes, the Pioneer Valley out there in Western Massachusetts," she said as we walked, suggesting she had treated a lot of patients like Jonathan from that green valley surrounded by rolling hills.

We had about 45 minutes.

I tried to push Jonathan to make some choices then, to think about another inpatient center, to focus on the horizon. I wanted Jonathan to seize his own destiny, create his own story, surface up from the haunting undertow of heroin addiction. I still believed it could happen, although I suppose I was less optimistic than I had been. But after a few minutes, with Jonathan tolerant but unmoved, Dr. Fine broke in. "It's too early for Jonathan to make any crucial decisions," he reminded me as he began to take over the discussion. "He needs to clear his mind. Perhaps in a few days he can decide what he wants to do next."

Although Fine didn't mention it, he must have thought I was too willful, too insistent in that hospital room, counterproductive in my desire. Before we left, I hugged Jonathan. "I love you very much," I told him.

We would talk the next few days over the phone.

I felt uneasy about the way our visit had unfolded as I hustled across the street to a coffee shop with Dr. Fine to get his view of Jonathan's predicament. Settling in across the formica table, he reassured me: "Except for the typical Jewish neurosis," as he jokingly put it, "there's nothing particularly wrong with Jonathan's psyche, although heroin is a complex and difficult drug."

Heroin addiction has a strong chemical foundation; whether it also has a strong psychological base is less certain, although environment and personality surely play important roles. If we are going to control chemical addiction, we need research to discover the appropriate drugs to counter it. The usual analogy here, Dr. Fine explained over coffee, far from perfect but helpful in this context, is insulin for diabetes. "We don't blame a patient for contracting diabetes. We do try to control the diabetes through insulin."

In the same sense, we cannot blame the heroin addict for his condition. We need to find drugs that can control it. Some people are no doubt more prone to addiction than others, probably through genetic coding. Jonathan was high-risk.

After leaving Jonathan and Dr. Fine that afternoon, I thought about heading home to Linda. They would not allow me to see Jonathan again, and he needed time on his own anyway. For me, the battle had turned. I was less certain Jonathan could recover quickly, but knew he needed to live in a safe environment while he worked through his addiction.

But did such an environment exist? Was there a safe place in a world where death stalked all of us despite our best efforts to hide from it, to trick it, to beat it? Death lurked in the very cells of human desire. I could hear it rustling.

Santiago and Endurance

I wanted to know why.

William Burroughs had put it this way back in 1953: "The question is frequently asked: Why does a man become a drug addict? The answer is that he usually does not intend to become an addict. You don't wake up one morning and decide to be a drug addict."

I remember once talking to Jonathan about how difficult it must be to stop taking drugs once you are in the cycle, how heroin must send people to some other place difficult to return from, how dangerous and disease-ridden such a journey must be. But I didn't want to let him off the hook. Even addicts have a choice, I claimed, once they're clean. Doesn't the addict have the power to choose?

I'd like to believe it, but this is an unfair argument, hard to hold on to. In fact, when pressed I don't buy it. Yet I have based my life on the assumption we can create our own lives, we are free, meaning comes from making choices. Our lives become the stories we create, the turns in the road we choose. That is our freedom, the mark of our human identity.

A nationally known alternative sentencing program I've helped create for criminal offenders, *Changing Lives Through Literature,* runs on a similar foundation. Back in the 1980s I had received a National Endowment for the Humanities grant to participate in a seminar at Princeton on the topic of literature and society. The focus of much of our discussion that summer was on the role of literature in a society becoming increasingly fascinated by technology and the business of science. Was literature doomed to a place, at best, at the margins of this society? Had a belief in stories become as remote from the center of our consciousness as a faith in ancient religion?

I was not willing to give up my old-fashioned commitment to the magic of a good story. To me, those stories about Cowboy Jonathan I told at bedtime were more central to human purpose than all the visual images speeding across the computer screens. I remained convinced through that long summer that literature provided the most important path back to the deepest meaning of our humanity.

Almost ten years later, I approached my good friend Bob Kane, a district court judge working in New Bedford at the time. Literature can make a difference, I told him. "I'd like you to take eight to ten criminals headed to jail and send them instead to a series of literature discussions at the university," I threw out as a challenge. "I'll get the seminar room and facilitate the discussions."

So we started the program. And it works. It has expanded throughout the country, cutting deeply into recidivism rates, demonstrating clearly the power of literature to change lives. Judges, prosecutors, legislators are on board with it today.

Yet I am not convinced that the heroin addict can make a strictly rational choice. Demons surround him, seduce him, call to him. He needs the power of God, salvation.

I didn't put it this way to Jonathan at the time. I only suggested that once an addict was clean, he should be able to make a rational choice not to use drugs again. Why would anyone choose to take drugs at that point? I asked him. It was not a question with a moral slant. I genuinely wanted to know.

Jonathan had no answer for me that day, not one he wanted to articulate anyway. He shrugged a little in response, made a face suggesting I just didn't quite understand.

I did understand, though. It's an illusion to believe rational thinking alone can carry us back home after we have journeyed out into the wilderness as Jonathan had.

One evening, a few weeks after discussing Hemingway's *Old Man and the Sea,* a student in my criminal offenders program talked about an experience he had had. He recalled how Santiago had endured depression in his lonely shack at night, how as a fisherman the old man had struggled against failure and loss, how he had overcome the excruciating pain in his body. Then be told us how he had walked down near his old neighborhood in New Bedford, tormented by his own frightening troubles, ready to recant a year-long vow of resisting drugs. He could hear the song of his old buddies as he came to the corner, anxious to make a turn off main street in the downtown area, drawn to the side street of siren voices.

But before he made the fatal turn that day, he heard another voice, the voice of Santiago, the old man. It was as if Santiago had become his friend, a character from literature now living forever in his heart. As he thought of Santiago, and the suffering the old man had weathered, the student decided not to turn the corner that day. He sauntered instead straight down the main street of the old whaling town. No guarantee that he would always do it that way, but at least for that day the fisherman endured. Santiago had been his salvation.

It was not rational choice exactly, but rather the power of imagination keeping my student from the devil. It was literature calling him to redemption.

Jonathan too needed to be redeemed.

Part Three

Heading West

When he entered Roosevelt, Jonathan insisted he didn't need further inpatient treatment, that he wouldn't go back to any institution for drug addiction. He had made similar assertions at Hazelden, though, and had agreed to go to a halfway house in the end. Finally, working the phones from Roosevelt near the end of his ten-day detox there, he found a spot he seemed satisfied with just outside of Palm Springs in California. It was for men only, with about eighteen beds, owned and run by a Jewish woman who had lost a son to heroin. It was called Michael's House in memory of her son.

Linda and I weren't happy about Jonathan's decision to travel to California, although, as Dr. Fine pointed out, Jonathan had found the place and made the arrangements with his own volition, a positive step, one imagined. California seemed too distant from home, too much the last refuge for desperate men. But we ramped up for another battle with Greensprings over the cost of Jonathan's care, a battle we would lose this time. And we bought him a round-trip ticket, open-ended for one year.

Michael's House was set up for long-term care, six months or so, but it sounded as if it had the virtue of flexibility and informality. We hoped this move westward would mark a new beginning for Jonathan.

The Saturday night before Jonathan was scheduled to leave Roosevelt, I drove to New York with Jeremy, went to the Carnegie Deli for a sandwich as we always did, father and son, again thinking Jewish thoughts over a pastrami and rye, half-sour pickles, and cream soda. Then we walked back to our hotel room at the Sheraton, the same Sheraton I had stayed in with Jonathan, sleeping there the best we could that restless night.

When we arrived at the entrance to Roosevelt the next morning around ten, we thought we'd have to wait for Jonathan to be released, but he was already checked out, standing with his bag next to him in a nearly empty lobby, ready with open arms to greet us.

He must have felt almost free for the moment as he stood there without any rules imposed on him. He could have bolted then, just as he could have run many times before, especially when he was out in the open like this, space stretching endlessly before him. But he didn't. I like to believe he wanted to work through his program, make it meaningful, snap his addiction, prepare for a new adventure. That's why he didn't take off. But I also imagine he didn't want to disappoint us. He cared. He couldn't just get up and run for it when he knew we were coming. And where was he going to go anyway? He had no money and found it difficult these days to work at a routine job.

We spotted him in the lobby, embraced, took him across the street for breakfast. It was a dismal Sunday morning in New York, overcast, few people on the streets. I was irritable, I am sure, bothered by the homeless sleeping on the sidewalk next to the wall of Roosevelt, concerned about Jonathan's confused situation, anxious about taking him to LaGuardia to see him fly away again.

I couldn't look at the homeless that day, although I am usually critical of all those good citizens who tend to turn away from the margins. For Jonathan, by contrast, the homeless were like scholar gypsies, harboring a secret knowledge he seemed to understand, or at least be fascinated by, a knowledge acquired long before "this strange disease of modern life, with its sick hurry, its divided aims, its head o'er taxed, its palsied hearts, was rife," as Matthew Arnold put it so long ago.

Right after breakfast we left Manhattan, drove toward the airport. Jonathan asked me to call Linda on the car phone, and I did. No doubt he wanted to speak with her, but he was also eager just to use the phone. He seemed like a little boy delighted with a new toy when I dialed the number for him. I was struck by his innocence as he began to talk to his mother with a broad and gentle smile beaming from his round face.

Once we checked into the airport and confirmed the flight, we had a long wait, over two hours. We bought soda at a food concession inside the terminal bustling with people en route, and then, sitting down, Jonathan took from his bag some books he wanted to show me as Jeremy wandered away for a while to be alone. He read a group of poems to me from one of his favorite writers, Charles Bukowski, rebel and barfly, alcoholic and hard-boiled visionary.

I don't remember which poems he read. I was hardly listening to the words, watching instead his brown eyes, tender and sweet, as the words flowed in a rhythmic stream:

> don't be ashamed of
> anything; I guess God meant it all
> like
> locks on
> doors

Bukowski wrote that at the end of his poem called "The Blackbirds are Rough Today." Perhaps Jonathan read that one to me.

Then Jonathan talked about a book Linda and I had given him, *To Be Loved*, an autobiography of Berry Gordy, the genius behind the music and magic of Motown. He admired Gordy's tenacity and determination, his struggles, and the largeness of his vision and his risks. "There's a poem by Rudyard Kipling that changed Gordy's life," he told me that day. It was a poem about manhood. Like Gordy, Jonathan was drawn to it.

He read it to me with passion that day at LaGuardia around a small wooden table near the crowded food concession stand. It was a moving poem, a poem I would read again, in part, at the unveiling of his tombstone.

The poem is classic Kipling, British manhood at its best, stiff upper lip, willful and daring. Not what you might expect from a young sensitive Jewish man, spiritual at times. The poem builds, takes on meaning:

If you can make one heap of all your winnings
And risk it on one turn of pitch and toss,
And lose, and start again at your beginnings
And never breathe a word about your loss...

And then at the end, if we've had any doubt, it makes its theme explicit.

If you can fill the unforgiving minute
With sixty seconds' worth of distance run,
Yours is the Earth and everything that's in it,
And—which is more—you'll be a man, my son.

That final phrase astounded me when I heard it: "you'll be a man, my son." Yes, Jonathan was a man in so many ways; yet he had a distance to run.

I agreed with Jonathan: It was a wonderful poem. Yet, as I think about it, it strikes me as a poem defining a male identity fundamentally different from what I believed Jonathan to be at his best. Berry Gordy, like Jonathan, had found inspiration there, and the poem is no doubt filled with male energy. But it defines a type of manhood drawn from British imperialism, the soldier, a variation on what will become the Hemingway hero, the Bukowski man. The poem does not celebrate the kind of manhood I have the deepest respect for, the mensch, the compassionate and caring figure facing the Cossacks in the shtetl, the Jewish man working to counter the brutality of the uniformed sadism of arrogance and power.

I wonder at the meaning Jonathan found in that poem. I recall, in a similar context, Jonathan mentioning how he admired Gordon Liddy—the ex-CIA agent and Watergate burglar, now turned talk show host—how he agreed with Liddy that we all should carry guns. That allusion, I assume, was just a moment of fleeting bravado on his part.

Jonathan read a lot of books this final year of his life. Was he looking for some secret knowledge from these books, some particular meaning? Did he enjoy the pleasure of reading, a temporary stay from the pleasure and pain of heroin? Did he read simply to pass the time, to move through that vast empty space, that burnt wilderness stretching endlessly before him? I can't find any pattern in his reading, any indication of direction or purpose. Yet he was reading, keeping his mind active, bathing himself in the cadence of human language, embracing texts like so many Jews in exile over the centuries. In one sense, he was doing what he had always done.

Near the very end of his life, Jonathan told me he had picked up a book on telecommunications. A few days earlier I had suggested he take advantage of his considerable talents in communication and look into that field. "Do you think I should attend technical school to learn the basics?" he asked. I couldn't tell if he was joking then, ironic in his tone, or if he was asking for guidance and advice, simple and straight forward. All I know is that I believed in him. He could accomplish anything if he could just concentrate and sustain his focus.

But Linda may have been right when she started talking about attention deficit disorder. "Maybe we should have Jonathan tested for ADD," she had said. "Often these situations need multiple diagnoses."

I wouldn't accept another category to imprison Jonathan in then, so I rejected the idea. Granted, Jonathan suffered emotional immaturity. He couldn't sustain long periods of concentration on a topic or a job this last year. That may very well be a characteristic of a sparkler. Some would say it has its advantages in this postmodern world, where we are bombarded by fragmented information, overwhelmed with endless images. Yes, possibly, Jonathan would never again be able to build a meaningful life within the boundaries of conventional living, never again be able to settle down in a routine existence. I only wish he had the option.

Jeremy and I walked with Jonathan to the gate at LaGuardia that day. His plane was ready to take off for California. We didn't know it then, but it would be the last time Jeremy would see his brother. We bought Jonathan a few magazines at a newsstand just before he left, watched him board the plane, saw it taxi out across the runway. It rose in the air finally, soared into the billowing clouds, vanished before our eyes. We couldn't leave the terminal for a while after that. We stared at the posted schedules on the electronic screens, shuffled around, but couldn't really move. Finally we walked together straight out the door and returned home to Dartmouth.

Michael's House and Manhood

*G*reensprings was as consistent as ever as we tried to convince them that under their contract they were required to pay for Jonathan's treatment at Michael's House. I called our contact in Pennsylvania, Deb Beck, the advocate so helpful in our battle over payment to Hazelden, but this time no one was able to get Greensprings to budge.

I suppose we were getting tired of the struggle, perhaps less protective of Jonathan, wishing he could find the strength within himself to continue. We asked him to talk with Greensprings directly. He called the case manager there.

"You should have heard him," Jonathan said to us on the phone from Michael's House later that day. "He told me the whole idea of treatment for addicts was one big waste of time and money. It doesn't work."

It is, I am sure, horrifying to listen to this kind of cynicism from the command post of bureaucratic control, especially when you are vulnerable, the human heart beating and exposed in the midst of a battle with drugs. That cynicism robs you of hope, all you have left for redemption. I can still hear the trembling in Jonathan's voice when he told us the story.

As it turned out, Jonathan was soon thrown out of Michael's House anyway.

The call came around dinner time one week night while I was working to get one of the university's new off-campus sites running smoothly down on Cape Cod. Linda had taken the call and seemed traumatized when I first saw her sitting on the bed in tears when I got home.

"It's Jonathan," she said, her body heaving in the midst of sobs. "They're throwing him out."

I held her tight, resisting my own body's will to collapse.

~

Jonathan had told us he didn't like Michael's House. Too unstructured, he claimed. Nothing new going on in the group discussions. He didn't need further inpatient treatment, he said, only the exposure to the outside world, where he could test what he had learned; no more abstract lessons, just the difficult process of converting those abstractions into the experience of daily life.

I agreed with that argument, at least part of me did. Jonathan needed to move beyond the shelter of an inpatient program to see how well he could apply the lessons he knew so well in the abstract. I think he believed that too. He understood the risks, but wanted to see if he could live without drugs in the ordinary world. That's why he grew anxious whenever he had to leave a halfway house. He was uncertain if he could manage it, vulnerable, out in the open.

Yes, that was the dilemma. He had not wanted it this way, but it had happened. For him the outside world was a dangerous place, teeming with temptation, but it was also a place representing freedom.

But what kind of freedom could that have been? When he first retreated from the outside, giving up his secret in that second-rate motel in Queens, he had only one main connection with that outside world—heroin. It had become the focus of his attention, his life and his love, his sickness and his demon. It was his life's obsession; everything else had become a means to that end. Inside he would suffocate, protected by a bell jar of thin air. Outside, he could breathe freedom, but that freedom promised death. Strange to realize that now, long after his death. But it's the truth. Jonathan was trapped no matter what road he took. Heroin had imprisoned him. Heroin was everywhere in control.

Linda had seen Jonathan in the emergency room at Miriam Hospital lying on a gurney, his hand stretched, out of control, straining to reach up to the pay phone next to him, his fingers playing with the metal push button keys, trying to figure out a way to make a call to the outside, to his dealer. That was when she realized how tightly heroin had him in its grip, when heroin had become his only dream, inside and out, his only reality. Heroin was the connection to the outside that rooted him in, isolated him, finally destroyed him. He was living in the midst of a grand illusion, trapped.

Linda, the hard-headed mathematician, knew better than I did the brute power of this drug. She was convinced if Jonathan returned home he would be called away, back to the streets, plagued with drugs, eventually stealing and stripping us blind. Looking back on it, I always had faith in Jonathan. I refused to believe he would commit those nightmarish acts Linda dreamt about. He had stolen from his friends to get drug money, but he had never been so desperate, as far as I knew, to commit a dangerous criminal act. He had drawn a boundary there, the reason he had given himself up to us in that motel lobby in Queens.

Heroin was his quick connection, but Jonathan also desired a deeper connection with other people. He could not help but reach out to those in need any more than he could help but appreciate the passion of life, the beauty of the world surrounding him. That too had its cruel irony.

The story we heard that day from the California desert was a common one. Jonathan had gone into the town of Palm Springs with another patient at Michael's House, a man in his 40s, and they both had gotten drunk. Later he admitted he had also been searching for drug dealers in the streets, but had not been able to find any. When the two returned, they were both asked to pack their bags and get ready to leave the house.

I spoke to Jonathan on the phone early the following morning from my office at the university as he sat, on the other side of the line, with the owner and staff at Michael's House. Together we reviewed his plans.

"I've found another halfway house in San Francisco," he told me. "It's called Henry Ohloff."

Never comfortable with moments of departure, I was far from convinced. I pictured Jonathan boarding a bus, traveling for over twelve hours, through Los Angeles, arriving in San Francisco late that night. I told him as much.

"The staff at the Ohloff House promised they'd pick me up in San Francisco early tomorrow morning," Jonathan responded.

It was a plan fraught with pitfalls and dangers, I thought.

But Jonathan was confident. "It'll work out, Dad. I promise."

He was excited about going to San Francisco, a beautiful and peaceful city that often reminded us of Boston, a city with the style of the Grateful Dead, a city that had passed the first anti-drug laws in the United States back in 1875.

With Jonathan listening in, I talked to his counselor and the owner of Michael's House on their speaker phone that morning, made certain that the unused portion of the money we had sent for Jonathan's care would be used for the bus ticket and minimum pocket cash for the trip. I pictured Jonathan moving across the highway in the dark electricity of night, taking heroin, bolting the bus, exposed, on the outside, running.

As it turned out, he got to San Francisco safely and on time, checked into a motel by himself near the historic Fisherman's Wharf for the night, and was settled comfortably into the Ohloff House the following morning. As far as I know, he never took drugs or alcohol any time he lived as a resident in that house, a good six months at least.

Jonathan's buddy went back to Los Angeles. I wonder if he is still alive, if he thinks about Jonathan when he walks by a neighborhood bar downtown in the City of Angels. Near the end of his life, Jonathan seems to have gravitated toward older men, although there is no clear pattern there. They were like older brothers for him, mentors of a sort. These men were tough, Wild West types not particularly well educated or well read, but he hung around with them, feeling perhaps a need for their acknowledgment.

They seemed to carry with them what the poet Robert Bly likes to refer to as Zeus energy, a rugged and unshaven manhood lost in the rhythm of the twentieth century, a loss embodied in all the Dagwood Bumsteads of the world, all the fathers and husbands now considered silly or foolish.

Yes, they were men closer to Kipling's model of manhood, or Bukowski's, than to Woody Allen's, or Philip Roth's. They didn't help Jonathan as far as I can see. He was seeking validation through them for his flights beyond the boundaries of caution and good sense. He wanted evidence of a future for himself, evidence of men who had survived despite their wretched battle with addiction.

San Francisco: The Ohloff House

*J*onathan needed the space, the distance cross-country from Dartmouth to San Francisco, to make his bid for recovery. Finding the house on his own, choosing it by himself, helped him stretch toward the success he was clearly struggling to grasp. This was his project now, his responsibility—he owned it. Although we would still help him with the monthly payments, it was essentially his to succeed or not.

When Jonathan entered the Ohloff House, a large old mansion set in the hills of San Francisco, with sizable sitting areas on the main floor and numerous bedrooms upstairs, I felt more removed from him than I had before. The geographic distance contributed to that feeling; the long struggle throughout the year must also have been taking its emotional toll. I was still concerned about his welfare, eager to see him find meaningful work, willing to guide him and to sacrifice whatever was necessary to save him from the dismal swamp, but I didn't pursue his every move, didn't agonize over each gesture the way I had before.

Don't get me wrong though. I wasn't giving in to the common belief that I couldn't control his destiny. Despite the best advice from professionals and friends, I refused to accept that limited role. But I was beginning to realize I couldn't force him to change. He had to come to that recognition on his own.

The Ohloff House was different from the Hazelden Fellowship Club, and that too accounted for the change in mood, the reformed connection. There were strict rules about adhering to schedules, attending meetings, being on time. The laws were rigorous with little mercy for violators. Jonathan worked hard to follow the plan. He grew to appreciate the discipline. The house residents respected each other, interacted with each other within the restrictions, cared about each other, developed friendships. If someone broke the rules, though, they all felt a sense of duty to the law, not to the individual who violated it;

to the discipline of the rule, not to the beat of the blood. But they all worked hard on the program together.

We didn't see Jonathan for the next few months, although we spoke to him frequently on the phone. Yes, things are going well, he would tell us. Yes, I like the program. Yes, I like this city. Yes, I am working on getting a job.

He seemed to grow in confidence. "Did you hear how clear his voice was?" Linda would ask with tender expectation and a smile on her face as she hung up the phone. But we rarely heard from Jonathan's counselor and found it difficult to get updates on his progress. Unlike Hazelden, Ohloff seemed to work from a philosophy that focused exclusively on the members of the house; they had little time to talk to family or friends outside. We did hear Jonathan was making headway, although he lost attention in groups at times, still distracted.

Occasionally I stayed on top of him with the full intensity of the old battle. "Jonathan, I'll take some time off when you get out," I told him. "We can get an apartment, anywhere you want, just until you get settled. I could help you find a job."

I was serious.

But he quickly refused such suggestions, laughing them off.

On the whole, I was more resigned, calmer perhaps, tired of the struggle, tired of all the talk and programs. At times Jonathan felt that way too. He was fed up with the life of recovery; he wanted it to end. He wanted a life different from the one he was trapped in.

In May, about three months after Jonathan entered the Ohloff House, Linda and I started attending NarAnon family meetings every Tuesday night, a group of middle-aged parents like ourselves, mainly from the Rhode Island area. There were usually a couple of dozen people there, more women than men, ready each week to exchange personal stories, to recite from the book of daily meditations, to drink coffee at the end of the evening.

I sat around the long folding table, listened quietly to their troubles, entered the conversation when it was my turn, but I couldn't connect, although the voices were friendly and caring, compassion filled with the cadence of pain. Linda drew more from these discussions and contributed more with her straight talk. She was eager to get there on Tuesday nights, and Jonathan was pleased.

"How're the meetings going?" he would ask us on the phone. No doubt he felt shame whenever he considered the turmoil he had caused within the family. But he liked the idea these groups might help the whole family and give us something to share in common, to discuss together. It was his culture, in a sense. He was the expert who could offer us insight and advice.

It was tricky business.

I never mentioned to Jonathan my own skepticism about these groups, and he never suggested they were silly or empty of meaning. The discussions to me were filled with chatter, but talking and listening, being involved in the rhythm of language itself, exchanging life stories, clearly had some therapeutic value. Jonathan may have been tired, but he had not given up. He never said a negative word about the groups. He was growing increasingly dedicated and serene, committed to the process in San Francisco, a loyal member of the Ohloff House.

The Beats

Five years have passed; five summers, with the length
Of five long winters! and again I hear
These waters, rolling from their mountain-springs
With a soft inland murmur.

*I*t was over five years ago when Linda and I traveled to San Francisco to see Jonathan for the last time. We didn't know it would be the last time then, of course, nor did we imagine that his brother Jeremy, agonizing through all this as a junior at Tufts, would be taking the bar exam for lawyers and celebrating a birthday, his 26th, five years later, the same age Jonathan was when he died.

If Jonathan was frightened about the future, he kept it to himself while we were out in San Francisco. He was sitting on a couch when we arrived, patiently waiting for us in the hotel lobby, an admirable trait of his character, always on schedule, rarely a hint of arrogance or anger in his look. He acted as the master tour guide without need for a map, the premier host who knew the city intimately, whose fondest pleasure was showing us the sights. He was determined that we have a good time and, like a gentleman with urbane wit and sophistication, he did all he could to make us, his guests, feel comfortable and welcome in his city. Jonathan was a man in San Francisco—imperfect but, on the whole, balanced and mature.

We took a long, leisurely stroll through the streets, from the historic wharf to North Beach and Chinatown all the way downtown to our hotel. We went to the City Lights Bookstore, and Jonathan and I climbed upstairs where all the books of the Beat writers, with their black and white covers, were kept. I remembered the store from those hectic days in the 60s when I had traveled with another student cross-country in a Volkswagen bug while an undergraduate at Brown, and recalled the wild times in Walla Walla when Jonathan was just five years old and those icons of the 60s, Allen Ginsberg and Ken Kesey, had come to our house as part of their visit to Whitman College, where I taught that year.

We took the books from the shelves that day, Jonathan and I, leafed through them one at a time, lingered over them together. Jonathan knew I loved browsing in bookstores, especially this one. I loved being there with him.

"Look at this book, Jonathan," I kept saying to him. "Remember when Ginsberg visited us at Whitman College? Jeremy was just a baby. Remember when Kesey splattered spaghetti all over the ceiling in our kitchen in Walla Walla when he cooked supper for us? I don't think Mom was too pleased with that. Jonathan, it makes me so happy to be here with you."

I must have sounded like a broken record to him. But he was so patient then, so understanding.

Later that day, the three of us ate dim sum upstairs in a restaurant in Chinatown, stopped across from a park in North Beach at an espresso bar with a brand-new Internet hookup for customers, took a cable car down the San Francisco hills from the heart of downtown to the tip of the waterfront, sipped chowder in a sourdough bowl at one of the stands on the wharf, and then watched Jonathan head back to the halfway house for a scheduled meeting.

It was a lovely day, thanks to Jonathan our host, a picture-book day from a family album.

I think often of our trip to San Francisco to visit Jonathan for that last time. Driving up to the hotel and seeing Jonathan, the smile and sparkle in his eyes reflecting his happiness in seeing us. That trip for me was a good one. I know it was not the same for Bob, but I felt Jonathan was clearer and more rational than he had been in a year. He knew San Francisco in and out. We spent the time walking, talking, sightseeing, and even planning for the future. Jonathan was listening again, sometimes even seeking advice.

~

The next day we took a boat out to Alcatraz. It was hot, the city was in the midst of a heat wave. I was agitated by the prison, its empty and desolate cells, by the heat, by my growing fear that things were not as good as they appeared. The prison itself reminded me of Jonathan's plight.

Linda was confident and optimistic, but I was growing less certain.

When we got back to the hotel that afternoon, Linda and Jonathan decided to go over to Golden Gate Park and then to shop together for a piece of luggage to replace one the airline had lost on the flight out. I stayed behind, waiting to meet them at an Italian restaurant where we had made reservations for 5:30 PM.

The talk at the restaurant was clear and calm that evening, restrained, catching the cadence of a nice meal, a pleasant past. I wish now we had made it more of a celebration, a special event. It was our wedding anniversary, June 25th. Linda and I had been married twenty-eight years. It was the last meal we would ever share with Jonathan.

I wish we had talked about other matters that night, given that meal a vitality, a memorable beat matching the passion of the life Jonathan had lived and embodied at his best. We talked about his group in the house, about his recovery, about the mundane process that supposedly would make him healthy if he took it slowly, one day at a time. I felt as if I were drowning in the soft waves of endless chatter, trying to hold Jonathan above the undertow.

We should have gone to a premier restaurant, celebrated the pulse and intensity of life as he dreamed it, howled around the city until dawn like Kerouac and Ginsberg had done, screamed about ultimate matters, listened to jazz music, joked and laughed until daybreak, and then gone back to the Ohloff House, picked up his bag, and headed out into the wilderness. And if he refused, yes, if he refused, I should have insisted, yelled to him that I was not going anywhere until he came with me. But, in the end, reason won out, the reasonable forces, the boundaries and the rules of pragmatic life as we had grown to know it.

We drove quietly through the streets of San Francisco that night in our small rental car, through the neighborhoods, slowly without stopping, and finally arrived back at the Ohloff House where we dropped Jonathan off. We had not planned to see him again on that trip, but when we discovered he had left his coat in our hotel room, we drove one last time to the house the following morning before heading to the airport. We wanted to make sure he had a coat in case he got cold.

We called to tell him we were coming just to drop the coat off and then would be going directly to the airport. We knew he was planning to meet a union organizer around 9:00 AM at the house, so we didn't plan to stay but a minute. When we got there, Linda sat in the car as I walked up the stone stairs to the house set on a steep hill on a large corner lot. Jonathan was in the front hall, waiting. For some reason he seemed surprised to see me. He took the coat, and I told him Linda was in the car. He immediately started walking out of the hallway down the stairs to see her. At the car, I hugged him and told him I loved him. He kissed Linda good-bye and then turned, walked back up the long set of stairs, disappeared into the inside hallway to wait for his appointment.

We never saw him again.

The Phone Call

Jonathan had made plans to live with Steve Johnson, an alcoholic and ex–Navy Seal, when he moved out of the Ohloff House. Steve's mother worried he would be living with a heroin addict, but Jonathan thought they would make a good match. They could take care of each other. "Will you keep beer in the new apartment?" I once asked Jonathan. "No, that wouldn't be fair to Steve," he replied. That reflected the check and balance they were both hoping for.

Originally Steve was scheduled to leave the house a few weeks before Jonathan and live with his sister until Jonathan got out. Then they would get a place together. As the plan developed, it changed, as such plans often do. Steve decided to stay until Jonathan was ready. Jonathan seemed pleased with the decision. I think he felt Steve cared about him, was willing to wait. The plan was complete; the future was settled and sealed. That must have given Jonathan comfort.

Jonathan sounded upbeat on the phone throughout July, and it was obvious Linda felt less hassled, more content, although we continued to go to the weekly group meetings and Linda found added relief with a female therapist in Rhode Island.

Jonathan practiced the rituals for leaving the house and rejoining the outside world. He went out for a final dinner with his group, got settled in his new apartment on Nevada Street, bought an answering machine, recorded his disembodied voice on the tape, and seemed in general to be on a track to success as he anxiously made the transition. I didn't hear much about those final rituals, though, no detailed account of the last night with the group, for example. Perhaps that's the way it should have been, given the tone and philosophy of The Ohloff House. Jonathan used to give us detailed accounts of such experiences, but now they were too predictable, I suppose, too standardized to tell about. They were part of an old story, and we were all wishing for a new one.

I didn't press Jonathan near the end, just listened to whatever he said, encouraged him when I saw an opening, accepted his telling and his not telling without interfering with his language, without bending his words to create a different story than the one he was focused on. I must have believed he was going to be all right. I must have been fooled by the assumption that keeping a distance was best. I am sorry I believed that, if I did.

When he left the Ohloff House, Jonathan worked, as he had in New York, in a telemarketing office. Phone surveys. A backroom operation. Cold calls into homes from a list on white paper. It was a low-paying job, but given his verbal skills it was the kind of work he could do easily and well. He also started to see a female therapist who conducted one long session with him, one he reviewed with us over the phone with a spark of rejuvenated energy.

"She said she'd like to meet with the whole family after a few sessions," Jonathan told me, his voice anxious but ringing with pleasure. "Do you think we could do that?"

Jonathan had good control over the use of money now too. We felt safe sending him checks for rent deposits, and when he heard there was a refund check from the IRS for several hundred dollars waiting for him in Amherst, he seemed happy enough to let us hold it for him.

The last time I spoke to him on the phone was the Sunday before he died. I detected a change in his voice, although Linda denied hearing it. To me he sounded restless, on edge, jumpy. He had an offer to work for a few weeks on an organizing campaign with a union, he told me, but it wasn't clear whether it would turn into anything permanent. It was difficult for him to get around on the bus. He needed a car. The Nevada Street neighborhood was too far from the center of San Francisco. He had seen some friends in Berkeley, and that neighborhood seemed more appealing. Maybe he should move there.

I didn't respond much to this report, half query and half lament, other than to suggest he should stay where he was for the time being, until he felt grounded, back on his feet, balanced in the world. On the whole, Jonathan appeared reasonable and disciplined, despite the jumpy undertone, not willful or purposely annoying. I was disturbed for the moment, but had to believe he was going to be all right.

When Jonathan didn't call by the end of the week, I started thinking about calling him. I didn't want to press him, but I was concerned. When I mentioned it to Linda, she responded as she often did. "If you feel like calling you should. Otherwise, you should keep quiet."

She didn't want to discuss it, I guess.

I finally did call on Sunday evening. I heard his voice on the answering machine, and left a message to call when he had a chance.

I know now Jonathan got that message. It was the last time he heard my voice, filtered through a technological maze. I know now he was on heroin when he listened to it, and he never called back. After Jonathan died, his roommate told me Jonathan had mentioned he had to call his mom and dad. He had called his brother Jeremy the night before in Somerville, but Jeremy had been out. He chatted on the phone that night with Jeremy's roommate about one of those fleeting problems younger brothers often have, one that older brothers can often resolve. Jonathan loved Jeremy; he was his adviser and best friend.

I wish I had said on that final message that we all loved him. I almost did, but then I worried his roommate would hear the message. So I left it unsaid. It wouldn't have made a difference, I suppose.

It was around 4:00AM when the phone rang next to my bed, the call we hoped would never come, the call I had feared since the beginning.

—Is this Mr. Waxler?

—Yes

—This is the medical examiner in San Francisco.

—Yes

—I am sorry but I have bad news.

—Yes

—Your son Jonathan died tonight.

I think we talked for a few more minutes, perhaps a few seconds. I stood at the edge of our king size bed, half leaning against it, listening to this strange voice on the phone telling me the worst news any parent could imagine. Then I sank down on the soft mattress, barely hearing him any longer. "I'm sorry but I'll have to call you back," I whispered.

His name was Graham Cowley. He had a southern accent.

Suddenly, out in the living room, trying to explain to Linda what I had just heard, I could sense the knot of grief already tightening in my body. Jeremy was visiting from college. He came from his bedroom and joined us on the couch, the three of us in shock and sorrow.

Looking out through the living room window into that raven night, I had no idea what to do except embrace Linda and Jeremy. It was as if we had stepped into the grave with Jonathan; only the lamp in the room, like a memorial candle, offered a trace of light.

Jeremy returned to his room to be alone, and after an hour or two it was obvious we had no choice; we had to get organized. And so, slowly, as if in a Chagall painting, we drifted, silently, just above the ground.

A phone call in the middle of the night. Usually these calls are the wrong number. But this one was different. Bob answered— answered like he had answered that call a year before that told us about Jonathan's struggle. This time Bob kept talking, and I knew what it was. It was the call we had been dreading since that first call. It was the call that no parent should get. I screamed, "Hang up the phone—he's wrong—he has the wrong person."

Talking to the Roommate

I spoke to Steve Johnson a couple of times that day. He had trouble talking through his own pain and tears. "Jonathan was a wonderful guy, warm and compassionate," he said. Yes, a mensch, I thought.

Early that night Jonathan had gone into his bedroom, Steve told me, the bedroom with posters of Chavez and Garcia on the wall. "After a while, I asked him how he was doing," Steve said. "I'm doing all right," Jonathan apparently replied. "Had a couple of beers, that's all."

"He even mentioned he owed you a call."

Steve regretted going out that night, he began to explain to me. And then it emerged—the ultimate irony, compassionate and cruel in its implications.

"There was another guy living with us in the house," Steve began, his voice stumbling as he talked. "Jonathan had been the one who convinced me...to let this guy live with us...just for a short time. We knew him from the Ohloff House....That's the way Jonathan always was. He wanted to help everyone....If he hadn't been living with us....I'm sorry, I have to hang up right now."

Yes, perhaps—perhaps then—oh yes, if it had only been different, if it had only been otherwise.

Steve didn't know Jonathan would die that night, of course. If he had, he would have stayed there with him, I am sure. I wish he had.

"If a person is near death, it is forbidden to leave him, so he should not die alone," the *Shulchan Aruch* tells us.

The next day, when I called him again, Steve was still troubled, but straightforward. Jonathan had been taking drugs for the last two weeks. On Wednesday he had been particularly bad. Steve knew who had sold the drugs to Jonathan: Pete, who had targeted Jonathan as an addict. Steve knew where Pete was. He was going after him to get him once and for all.

I wondered if this was why Jonathan had wanted to leave the neighborhood, move to Berkeley, begin to hang out with a new group of friends. I wondered if we should go after Pete, have him arrested, thrown in jail for murder.

Whatever Cannot be Grasped is Eternal

I don't want to make Jonathan in death more than he was in life. But I want him to be remembered for the man I know he was. At his bar-mitzvah, the Rabbi talked about his special spark, a spark, according to Jewish tradition, that connects all our souls, that can emerge from the dust into a flame of wonder and goodness. Jonathan deserves to be remembered for what he accomplished in his brief life. The terrifying journey he took us through the last year of his life does not negate his accomplishments. He was a man who deserves our honor and respect. Jonathan was up against a hard game. He had to die to beat it.

> *Whoever degrades another degrades me,*
> *And whatever is done or said, returns to me.*

Later, a year later, Jeremy, his only brother, preparing for law school, would write the following—perhaps thinking as he wrote about the bruises on his knees and elbows from the times that Jonathan brought him out onto the concrete parking lot in the back of our apartment complex in New Bedford and pushed him on his new bicycle straight out across that vast wilderness as he yelled "pedal, Jeremy, pedal"; or perhaps thinking as he wrote about the sign on Jonathan's bedroom door when we lived in the raised ranch in Dartmouth, before the fir trees were planted in the backyard, the sign written in magic marker that read "Keep Out" because his big brother was studying and had just had a lock put on, so Jeremy wouldn't again race in and jump all over him, wouldn't challenge his big brother again to a world-wide wrestling match; or perhaps thinking, as he wrote in his loneliness, about the digital clocks that twice a day read 8:20 throughout the world, 8-20, the number that serves as an endless reminder of the worst day in Jeremy's life, the day he lost his big brother and confidant, his best friend, forever.

Unfortunately, the most harrowing experience of my life has given me purpose and direction. I wish it had been different. Last year, after a long battle with heroin addiction, my only brother Jonathan died. I am still grieving. I know that my life will never be the same. I have lost my brother and my best friend.

Before his death, I took life for granted. Now, although I grow angry and then sad knowing that I must live with this tragedy forever, I believe that life is precious and that I must seize the opportunities before me because I may never get another chance. My brother's death has taught me the value and possibilities of the smallest details in life. It has taught me to endure hardship and to be aggressive. Thanks to my brother Jonathan, I see the world with new eyes.

Everyday I think of the tragic struggle of my brother, but I also reflect on the good fortunes of my own life. Although I have become increasingly pessimistic about "the war on drugs" and the future of many young adults, I have become increasingly optimistic about the possibilities for finding meaning in the small acts of daily life. New chances and opportunities appear to me where I could never see them before. As a result, I try to make it easy for others to celebrate their own lives. I try to be pleasant to everyone around me and treat everyone with respect because I am convinced that every human being deserves a chance to live a life of dignity and caring.

Ironically, my brother's death has helped me to grow certain of my decision to go to law school. In a way, a part of me died when Jonathan died, but instead of burying myself, I have been rejuvenated. I take nothing for granted and work relentlessly to achieve all of my goals. Law school was only a possibility for years, but nowadays, with a clearer perspective on life, I can see that law school is of central importance to me. It will make a difference to me and enable me to make a difference for others.

It amazes me that I used to worry about how I would ever find time to make my bed or to watch a football game on TV. At times I was obsessed with the apparent weight of those matters. Nowadays I focus on what I can do to better myself and to help others around me. I realize that there is not enough time in life to worry about every minor matter. I need to contribute and grow. For me, law school is the next important step in my life. My brother's death leaves me without doubt about that. It is precisely what I want to do. It will help me to help others.

During my first two years in college, I never grappled with the meaning and importance of life. I had little sense of direction and purpose. When, in my junior year, I learned that my brother suffered from heroin addiction, I was reminded of how precious life really is. Working hard and achieving goals became very important in my life. I took on two internships and boosted my grades in my courses at Tufts the final two years. Nowadays I strive to create meaning for my life whether at work or at the gym or with my friends.

My brother was the most wonderful person I have ever known. He died from a horrible disease that we cannot seem to cure. He had recently finished his M.A. in labor studies and dreamed of going to law school, but he never got the chance. He didn't believe he would die because, I imagine, he thought he was invincible. I watched him engage in a valiant struggle to break his addiction, but it was much too powerful. He wanted to live a normal life and take advantage of the opportunities available to him, but his disease held him back. He deserved the best, but never got it. I see the chances that I have, and I plan to take full advantage of them. The tragedy of death has caused me to see the chances that stand before me in life.

There are deep lessons in sadness and grief. Jeremy knows that. Jonathan's loss changed all of us. Heroin addiction is a family affair. One hopes it made us better people somehow.

~

Yes, of course, I wanted to protect Jonathan. But I couldn't. How could I? The world is a brutal place, and he needed to protect himself. If he had let someone love him, perhaps I could have protected him. A father should do that for a son. He did so much I admired; at times, I think he did it simply because I asked him to. But he was his own man, and that too I admired. He didn't believe in rules; he thought he could create his own.

Perhaps I should have judged him more severely. A father should be a judge, but I wanted him to create his own life, free from the restriction of my rules. He had enough rules to deal with, I thought. He needed structure imposed on him, granted; but for him, the weight of strict rules was as burdensome as a narrow jail cell. Jonathan wanted to travel with the gypsies; he wanted to be free.

At the top of the list he developed at Hazelden offering reasons not to take heroin, he wrote, "because I might die." Did he write it to satisfy his counselors or did he believe it? I wish I knew the answers to such questions.

Jonathan loved life, had a great appetite for it, yet his days had grown empty in this last year. He must have felt useless, needing to fill that long endless space with a heroin high. I should have tried to stay right on top of him, although I know that kind of control would have driven him insane. He needed to focus; we could have gotten clarity on that together. He needed a meaningful job; I could have helped him find one. He needed to be protected against the brutality of death, but there is no safe place in this world.

I wish he could have told me plainly why I was wrong when I suggested the choice in the end was his, whether to stay off drugs or not. Perhaps he didn't want the responsibility that goes with admitting that choice, but more likely, he knew that heroin craving is larger and more voracious than most of us can imagine.

Heroin addiction is not primarily a psychological habit but a physiological assault on the body. And it is always the body that betrays us in the end.

I will never know what was in Jonathan's mind that fatal day when he picked up heroin for the final time. He probably didn't know precisely what was in his mind either. I can't grasp Jonathan's life totally, and neither could he. Maybe that's the way it should be.

As the French poet Edmond Jabes reminds us, "Whatever cannot be grasped is eternal."

Jonathan Blake Waxler. He had passion.

Part Four

Funeral

*L*inda was anxious that I might want a large public funeral for Jonathan, but with little discussion we agreed to make the burial as private as possible, just immediate family. We also concluded, with little more than a nod, that the shiva ritual at our home, traditionally a week long, would be only a day or two. It was impossible to imagine Jonathan would not be with us, that he had disappeared forever.

With the help of my brother David, we began to make the required plans. I called my old friend in Cambridge, a retired rabbi, Bernie Glassman, to conduct the graveside ceremony, and talked to the coroner in San Francisco again and to the funeral director in Providence.

I was surprised when the coroner told me he planned to do an autopsy on Jonathan, an investigation required by law in such cases. I was hesitant, imagining no further need to tamper with Jonathan's body. But it seemed unreasonable to fight such a process and so, on reflection, I let it go.

Later I ordered a simple and unadorned casket made from pine for Jonathan's burial, in keeping with Jewish tradition. The funeral director called me the next day, asking why I hadn't told him how big Jonathan was. The original casket was too small, he said. He should get a larger one. I agreed.

I drove our green Buick LeSabre from our home to the Jewish cemetery near the local airport, Linda and Jeremy in the back seat, Rabbi Glassman in front next to me. The other family members followed close behind with their headlights on as we slowly wound our way out into the countryside.

"How did it happen that I am going to my own son's funeral?" I wondered. Rabbi Glassman had officiated at Jonathan's and Jeremy's bar-mitzvahs, so he knew them; he knew our family well. The two of us had founded the Center for Jewish Culture on the University of

Massachusetts, Dartmouth campus several years before and had spent a lot of time working together. He was a good man, a good speaker. But I can't remember anything he said at the grave.

At the end of the prayers, I gazed longingly at the wooden casket that had been lowered into the ground by a small machine. Everyone else had begun to move away, but I couldn't. I wanted to talk with Jonathan, be with him. It was only Jonathan I wanted to hear, only Jonathan I wanted to see. Finally my brother approached, like a ghost, and helped release me from the grave.

Shiva

"*D*o you realize people are lined up at the front door waiting to get in?" a man asked, trying to comfort me.

"Yes, I suppose that's what happens when a young person dies," I responded.

The two days of shiva, people flocked to our home. It was filled day and night with friends and colleagues offering condolences.

"Remember the wonderful gift that he was," a cantor counseled. "Linda will need your attention and help," someone else explained. "Take as much time as you need before returning to the university," a few suggested. "You should get back into the routine of work as soon as you can," others advised. It was comforting to have these people near me, but draining. It was good hearing human voices, although the advice offered seemed empty and meaningless.

After those two days, exhausted, I sat on the back porch of our raised ranch gazing at the fir trees casting looming shadows across the green grass, the trees Jonathan had planted. For hours I read and reflected, looking at books like *A Death in the Family*, a classic American novel by the Southern writer James Agee, and *Sayings of the Fathers*, a traditional Jewish text with poignant passages of spiritual insight. I wondered if I would ever be able to go back to my office and work as an administrator. The bustling world of work seemed remote to me, a distant dream. I was still floating.

But what choice did I have? I needed to move in some direction, resist the call from the grave. And so, about three weeks into it, I dragged myself back to the concrete buildings on the college campus and my job as Dean of Continuing Education.

People smiled. They were friendly and sympathetic. They came by my office, stood before my wooden desk, mouths opened as if they were screaming into silence. I knew they wanted to say something. But a plain linen shroud covered the world and separated me from them and from myself. I feared that even human language would shatter, like potter's ware, the skeleton of my fragile self.

It was difficult to talk, especially to people at large functions, crowds I didn't know. I sat in meetings, refusing to listen to discussions, wondering when the conversation would end so I could return to my office and close the door tight behind me. Linda and I didn't go out much either. It was impossible to mix with small chatter. It had been so easy before.

Starting Over

For me, work was a way of trying to stay alive, to survive. But for Linda, work was not an option that first year. She needed to be alone. Her mourning was clearly going to take a different shape from mine.

Linda believed if she could somehow keep secret Jonathan's death, then he wouldn't really be dead. Hers was a silence of a different order. She wanted to protect herself and Jonathan against the terrible truth she knew, and she needed to be alone to do that. Even later, when she was able to give his death a voice, it was still as if the secret should be held close. She didn't want to name it all at once. It needed to be revealed slowly, over many years, spoken in broken fragments, a little bit at a time.

As she put it in her journal, thinking about those first few months:

> When I enter a room filled with people I have not met, I think to myself "When will they ask THE QUESTION?" Years ago, when I was a college student, the standard question was "Where do you go to school? What are you majoring in?" Now the conversation seems to begin with "What do you do? Where are you from? How many children do you have?" Those are not difficult questions to answer ordinarily, but for me, it's different. I have two children. I will always have two children. Their pictures, testifying to their existence, are scattered throughout my home. So, when THE QUESTION comes up, I say, "Two sons." With the next question "How old are they?" I hesitate and hear myself saying "My son Jeremy is in his 20s. My son Jonathan died at the age of 26." My secret is out and I watch as the person struggles uncomfortably to find the right words to respond with or, more likely, the right moment to walk away.

Yes, we had been carried over a tremulous threshold no parent should ever approach. The math teacher and the professor of English Romantic poetry, dizzy and abject now, enveloped by an unsettling rhythm of time, struggling to map out a new geography of the self. Uncertain where we were headed, people seemed equally uncertain of us. We were like Jews in the wilderness, unable to define our place in the world or feel at home, yet seeking redemption.

I don't know how I got through those first months after my son, Jonathan Blake Waxler, died, although from one perspective, it doesn't really matter. My grief was all-consuming. Every ounce of my energy in those days went into surviving. I got through each day any way I could. I know now it's different for each bereaved person. Working or not working, watching meaningless television programs, viewing movies, cleaning, sleeping, crying, talking to people, not talking to people, answering phone calls, not answering phone calls, waiting until you are ready to call people back, looking at old pictures, remembering your child, pretending that your child is still alive—all this behavior is okay. We each have our own way of surviving and somehow we find that way, we must. But be assured of one thing. It is a long and lonely journey.

~

We had begun an interior journey into rugged terrain underground, cavernous and dark, shards and rubble everywhere, frightening and without end. We wouldn't admit it, though. Instead we set out for new physical locations, taking trips by ourselves a record number of times, avoiding traditional holiday gatherings, family, friends, the past.

During Passover, we went to New Orleans, a city sizzling with sensuous pleasure, mouth-watering temptations, hot music drifting through the humid air. It was an act of defiance as much as an act of survival. Breakfast at Brennan's—turtle soup, poached eggs on crisp fried trout with hollandaise sauce, bananas sauteed in butter, brown sugar, cinnamon, and liqueur flamed in rum over vanilla ice cream—"scandalously delicious," as the menu said. And, of course, later, warm beignets with café au lait (for those who like it that way), and, yes, creole jambalaya.

We listened to jazz and the blues, walked up and down Bourbon Street, stopped in at Preservation Hall, lingered at Jackson Square, rode the trolley up to St. Charles. In the French Quarter, we discovered a restaurant that served a dozen succulent raw oysters with beer at such a low price that we kept going back as if we had finally hit pay dirt. We were in the Big Easy, some other place.

It was only a fleeting dream though, caressing our soft flesh, but not penetrating the bruises deep in our soul. Bukowski, one of Jonathan's favorite writers, once said, "New Orleans was a place to hide," and I agree. For Linda and me, it was a place to hold tight to a secret.

I regret much of that trip to New Orleans now, especially missing the Passover celebration, a traditional time for family gathering around a Jewish table, a time for matzoh, not oysters, a time for ritual objects, not scandalous temptation, a time for moror, karpas, charoset, lamb shank, salt water, roasted egg, all placed on silver platters with symbolic devotion atop a white tablecloth waiting patiently for sacred wine and prayer.

Yes, Passover is the Jewish holiday for great symbolic stories, not Southern scandal. It is a reminder of the meaning of the covenant, of how first-born sons, like Jonathan, were saved from death by the blood of the paschal lamb, of how the journey of the Jews took them from Egypt to the Promised Land, from slavery to freedom, from exile to home.

This particular Passover was also the last Seder before my father died, the last opportunity to share the story around the table with him and the rest of the family. As the tradition commands: "Thou shalt tell thy sons."

But I was not there.

Yet the trips were necessary, I suppose, helpful as a dream always is. Linda and I were separate and distinct from the rest of the world, ghosts seeking a place of rest on the other side of the ordinary.

I wish friends from that ordinary world had been more considerate, more compassionate, more understanding. But I know their fears. They didn't want to be haunted by a father who had lost a son. That's too frightening. I grant them that.

"How's Linda doing? they asked me. "How's she holding up?" But they rarely asked about my feelings. Perhaps they were exploring indirectly, not wanting to make explicit inquiry about the feelings of the man of the house. Perhaps they were mindful of the Talmudic injunction about how the comforter should approach the mourner. "During the first twelve months, he may offer him words of consolation, but he may not inquire about his well-being."

Yes, they might have been looking for a hint about my emotional state by asking about Linda's. But most of them thought that as a husband and father I should be strong, should support and protect Linda and Jeremy— that was my job. I understand the stereotype. But I was haunted too. I was like the ancient jazzmen in Preservation Hall in the French Quarter, men playing music from some other world on their golden trumpets and old piano.

I wanted someone to acknowledge that.

The Ambiguity of Memory

*I*t was over three decades ago when I returned from Boston Lying-In hospital the day after Jonathan was born. All the neighbors in our brick apartment house on River Street in Hyde Park were working in the back of the building clearing mountains of snow from the parking lot that day after the blizzard in 1969. Exhausted and excited, I bounded out of the car to tell them my good news.

"I'm a new father," I shouted.

They didn't care. "Congratulations, buddy. Now grab a shovel and help us with this damn lot," they replied. "That storm really socked us in."

The ordinary world goes on, whether you're willing to join it or not. So Linda and I had to take care of the ordinary moments of daily life. The trick was how to give meaning to the memories of Jonathan mingled with the murmur of those moments. We had to close some of those memories out, seal them off with a trap door. Others had to be wrestled with, given depth, expanded.

Each time we received a notice about Jonathan in the mail from the IRS, or anywhere else, it was as if grief had been delivered to our front door. I asked a lawyer to help, but eventually went myself to the Probate Court in Taunton to get the forms necessary to transfer the money from Jonathan's accounts to Jeremy. That made sense. Easy enough at the surface. The finances demanded a sense of the end. Shut the door.

We set up a memorial prize for social justice in Jonathan's name. Each year an undergraduate student reflecting Jonathan's vision of social justice would be chosen to walk across the stage and receive the award in the main auditorium at the university during the honors convocation near the end of the spring semester. I asked both the director of the UMass Dartmouth Foundation, Don Ramsbottom, and an old friend and respected colleague in the English Department,

Richard Larschan, to help organize the giving. We collected enough donations to keep the award expanding indefinitely. Easy enough at the surface.

Our approach was practical but troubling, draining the little energy sustaining our bodies yet allowing us the illusion of progress. In fact, everything Linda and I did bore a complex ambiguity. Dashing to new places seemed refreshing, an immediate escape from the world we no longer fit into, but it also delivered a reminder of how distant we were from the world we had known, how tight the linen shroud gripped that world. Giving a prize in memory of Jonathan's vision of social justice kept him alive, but also echoed back his absence. Despite our bluff, there was no easy way out of this ambiguity, no simple way to untie the Gordian knot of grief.

Jonathan had changed our world forever.

I am not ashamed to tell you that I wept a lot during this period. But Linda's despair seemed deeper than my tears. It was as if she wanted to cleanse herself completely from the past but at the same time hold Jonathan's life and death close to her, keep him safe inside her.

That secret she held was like an embryo she was nurturing. Yes, she was carrying Jonathan in her body, protecting him from being thrown brutally into the world. She wanted to be alone with her innocent baby, and yet she felt so alone herself, an orphan abandoned by the world. I wanted to help her if I could, protect her.

It has been eight months since my beloved Jonathan died, and I continue to be overwhelmed with sadness and despair. Yet I want to put my finger on the exact triggers of these emotions. I am wondering what set me off after the return from our trip to New Orleans. We usually spend Passover together with family at home. But this year Bob and I had to get away. After we returned, I immediately started working on the few bonds and mutual funds that Jonathan had owned. I wanted to get rid of them, to put them into Jeremy's name, to get them off my mind. Of course, Jeremy doesn't want them. But who else would Jonathan want to have his assets? The more I worked on them though, the more upset I became. I guess that is what started this recent round of despair.

Now, just back from another trip, this time to Montreal—getting away from home seems to help a bit but the reentry is always cruel—the UMASS Dartmouth Honors Convocation and the social justice prize we will be giving in Jonathan's memory saturates my mind. No parent should ever have to give a prize in memory of their child and I wonder how I am going to get through the ceremony. I should be the proud mother, going to see her child receive an award, not the grieving one, going to watch an award being given so that her child will be remembered.

This was not part of my plan for life—I always figured things would go so smoothly. I feel alienated from everyone, bitter that the world goes on after such a tragedy, and no one really understands. My grief seems to wrap around me. I feel as if I am in a dark pit and I am haunted by those who hardly ever call to see how I am doing, by those who have completely abandoned me.

Therapists and Fierce Mother Love

Seeking the nurturing cadence of language—the Jewish hope in exile that words, texts, books alone can redeem us—I drove an hour each way for weekly visits to a psychiatrist, a woman with a small office outside Boston. I needed to try it, to see if I could work meaning through intense and focused discussion, the talking cure, as Freud had suggested. Finding language to shape my grief should give me comfort, I thought, although I knew the call of death could never be silenced.

"Within language lie concealed magic, forces of nature and history, lees of instinct and culture, a heritage of emotions, habits of thought, traditions of taste, inheritances of will—the Imperative of the Past," I read in a book on the Jewish canon by Ruth Wisse. To pursue language was to pursue Jonathan, keep him close to me, transform fate. I believed it. It was a way of placing myself back in the world, I thought.

I wouldn't avoid death on this path, but might rediscover purpose, language marking it out. "Words mark us as intensely as we mark them....And behind each of them, life, in its simplicity or complexity, menaced by death," the French poet says.

So I worked the talking cure with my psychiatirst in cramped quarters in her warm office, believing I was adjusting better than Linda was, as I struggled session after session to find in the sensuous rhythm of language the mysteries that marry life to death, that create connections beween fathers and sons, or that at least trace out a temporal home in exile.

"I had a dream last night, doctor," I told her one morning. "It still haunts me. I was watching from my window as construction workers down below were tearing up my driveway with a jackhammer so they could resurface the area. Suddenly one of them got badly injured. Laid out on a stretcher, he was carried from the driveway into my home. There was a party in the house, all sorts of people eating and talking, downstairs and up. I didn't know where to go or how to help as they brought the body of the man inside."

Linda went to a therapist as well, a woman in Providence with a master's degree in social work. We both wanted to help ourselves and each other and gain some insight into the unnatural experience of losing a child. Her journal reflects how much she wrestled with this mystery. There is a fierce attachment to Jonathan in her language, as well as an understandable bitterness and anger reflecting her fierce mother love, an anger that I never could muster.

> I was thinking yesterday about seeing Jonathan at Butler detox. "Please Jonathan," I begged. "Stay here and let us find the best help for you. If you refuse, I'm so afraid that you will die—I WILL NOT LET YOU DIE. I am your mother and I love you so much I can't bear to watch you do this to my child."

> I hate this—having to grieve. I hate having to be okay so I don't make other people uncomfortable with my sadness. And yet I end up being so bitter and feeling that no one really cares. Maybe I should go around crying and telling everyone how awful I feel and maybe that would help people know how to deal with me. I should probably ask people for help so I don't have to feel so resentful. But I find that so hard. I think they should be offering real help, not just lip service.

I can't comprehend Linda's ferocious mother love. It seems an emotion that fathers barely know, whether bound in the best of relations with their children or cut off in moments of deepest grief. Linda made it part of her flesh, holding Jonathan inside of her, refusing to let him out, not wanting her body to give birth to a corpse. The struggle made her physically sick, practically immobile.

I had never allowed my body this kind of exposure. I believed in the word, that the word must be made real, that texts provided the sensuous pleasure of life itself. I was part of the People of the Book, a believer in texts. For me, texts, and only texts, were my refuge, if not my redemption.

They were written into the flesh of the family bond, calling for the embrace of parents and children, fathers and sons.

Fathers and Sons

Yes, a father and son relationship is always difficult, I suppose. So much is at stake. A son represents the next generation, the hope of the family name, the dreams lived and the dreams deferred. If you develop a close relationship with your son, you believe you have shaped that life in some significant way. If you have not been close, you still have shaped that life through your absence, whether you admit it or not. I felt very close to Jonathan; his destiny was tied to mine, and I often believed if he disappeared, then I should too.

And what about a father? He is a crucial connection for the son to the past, to the roots of the son's identity as that identity grows into the future. The father is there to protect the son when necessary, to strengthen him through the difficult and thorny stretches of life. And in the modern American culture, where fathers too often yield to the vapid middle-class voices around them, the sons can reawaken passion and imagination. As Blake once put it:

> Father O Father what do we here
> In this Land of unbelief and fear
> The Land of Dreams is better far
> Above the light of the morning star.

My own father would die about two and a half years after Jonathan's death. He was in his early 90s, yet his death was still painful to me. I published the eulogy I gave at his funeral in the local newspaper a year after he died when we unveiled his gravestone. It was a fitting tribute from a son to a beloved father, something that my father dearly deserved. A number of people commented on it.

"I know it took a lot of courage to make your personal feelings public like that," one woman told me after class at the university one day. "I admire you so much for that."

"I had to come up and tell you how much I liked what you did," said a man hustling across the tennis court on another occasion. "I hope it serves as a model to remind other sons they should honor their fathers in similar ways."

Other readers, however, were mortified that a man would write such sentiment. Their response reminds me of the conflicted and troubled meaning of manhood in America, how we have constructed it, how we, as men, still fear expression of emotion in public places, how men don't cry.

The relationship between a father and son is never easy, but I know my father did all he could to help me, and I like to believe I did the same for Jonathan. After Jonathan died, my father was distraught. He came over to my house one afternoon about a week after the funeral. I was standing in our small kitchen, bent over the counter, clearly in despair.

He took me by the shoulders and shook me. "Snap out of it," he said. "You've got to snap out of it."

I was astonished. He was usually more sensitive than that, and I am sure he didn't mean that I should be hard-boiled, a man's man, only that I should try to move forward. After all, I was an important part of his future. I was his son.

A few days later he came by the house again, shortly after Linda and I had set up the social justice prize in Jonathan's memory at the university. I had suggested that he and my mother contribute to the fund to help keep Jonathan's vision alive. I was sitting in the backyard on the deck near the fir trees when he came in, still looking depressed and numb, I am sure.

"I don't know how much we should give to Jonathan's social justice prize," he began to tell me. "Mom and I have been discussing it."

He seemed genuinely baffled, caught between the American values of money and appearance and the deeper values, learned so long ago in the shtetl and through the legacy of family tradition.

He had often told me over a Friendly's cheeseburger, a melt as they called it, the story about his friend, the wealthy and well-respected president of the local bank, who had called him to appraise some property in New Bedford when he was still working fulltime as a real estate agent.

"I looked at that property, Bob," my father would always say, "and then went home that night. I couldn't sleep. The price he wanted me to write up for him was much too high. I called him the next day and told him I couldn't do the job. Didn't have time."

I would always nod then, and he would go on.

"He never asked me to do work for the bank again. I could have made a lot of money."

"I'm proud you did that, Dad," I would say as he looked in my eyes, seeking a sign. "It was the right thing to do."

He was not so certain, though. Did he fear the risk?—he always wondered. Was it moral strength or lack of guts that determined that choice?

"I did it for you two boys, you and your brother, and your mother," he would say.

And so I explained to him that day in my backyard what he clearly already knew, that I really didn't care how much he gave, that I had just lost one of the important treasures in my life, that was all I cared about right then.

As I looked over at my father, standing in the corner of my wooden deck splashed with sun that late August afternoon, he began to cry. Surprisingly, this man, who was often filled with pride, asked me to forgive him. He apologized, confessing he was confused, just as he had been confused at similar moments in his life, when he had, for example, called his younger brother Hymie to task during World War II for wearing his military uniform into a club where conventional suits and ties were the rule. Hymie, an Air Force sergeant, had died shortly afterwards, shot down leading his last scheduled bombing mission over Nazi Germany.

We walked together that day to his old skyblue Buick parked in my driveway at the side of the house, and I opened the door for him to get in. At some deep level, my father was remembering then the time of my own birth, a difficult time when he had left my mother in their Boston apartment on Commonwealth Avenue to mourn the death of his own mother and his youngest brother David. Both had died within a few days of each other in New Bedford, just before I was born on December 16, 1944, in a hospital across the Charles River in Cambridge. There were still tears in his eyes as I embraced him in the driveway that August day. And then he drove off, headed home to see my mother.

He had compassion, my father, and it came, I believe, from that disturbing image of arrogance he held in his mind from childhood, that image of brutality that he detested, the memory of Russian soldiers on horseback violently riding in the name of the Czar, demanding total obedience from the Jews in that small shtetl with streets of dirt tucked away in a green valley outside of Kiev. It was a traditional little town surrounded by what appeared, to my father's innocent imagination, to be lofty mountain peaks. My father always wanted to know what was beyond the horizon, on the other side of those rolling hills grown to mountains looming in his mind.

I am also sure now that this was why I always felt a spiritual bond sitting near him in our cosy den when I was a young boy, listening intently to Kate Smith at the end of her television broadcast in the 1950s, signing off for the night, singing her signature song, "When the Moon Comes Over the Mountain."

My father never read a novel, though. It was my mother, a proud convert to Judaism, thirteen years younger than my father, who brought me to books and to the love of literature. It was my mother, who grew up on a farm in the countryside in Dartmouth, who took me by the hand, walked me to the public library. It was my mother, with her light brown hair and sparkling blue eyes, who filled our house with books.

Social Justice

*H*ow was I able to present Jonathan's social justice award that first year at the honors convocation with over 400 people watching? I am amazed.

Somehow I did get out of my chair on that spring day, walk across the wooden platform, and hand the envelope with the $500 check to the recipient. I had been sitting on the stage with the other deans, watching the ceremony at a safe distance. Then I heard Jonathan's name called out in the cavernous auditorium packed that day with proud parents. "The Jonathan Blake Waxler Memorial Prize for Social Justice," the voice boomed through the air.

I know I got up then, because when I returned to my chair I glanced down at the crowd in their seats below me. Everything was out of focus, blurred. It was as if the world was damp with my tears, a prism of fragmented colors, in need of repair.

Linda believes she couldn't have done what I did that day, but I know she could have. A couple of years later, she would make an eloquent speech on stage at Dartmouth High School before giving a similar prize there. I doubt I could have done that. In her journal entry at the end of April that first spring, a few days after the first award ceremony, Linda describes her feelings:

> *Sunday, four days since the awards ceremony. The award was given out on Wednesday afternoon and it has taken me this long to recover. It was one of the hardest days of my life, and it's impossible for me to begin to explain to anyone how I felt. Thinking about it days in advance made me weep constantly, and when I hit the parking lot at UMASS and saw the parents going in to revel in their children's achievements, I did not know if I could walk into the building. How could I go in and hear my son's name announced, in memoriam? I saw a few people inside who told me how nice it*

was to honor Jonathan's memory—but I could only think that they, parents themselves, didn't understand how hard this day was for me. I find it hard to believe that Bob had the strength to go up on the stage before four hundred people and hand the award to the recipient, Rico. I was standing in the back of the auditorium crying, unable to hold back the tears despite the crowd of people around me.

Yet there was also a fire in the midst of that award ceremony. I want to note it. That fire, brimming with light, stretches from William Blake to Marge Piercy to Jonathan himself.

> We stand in the midst of the burning world
> primed to burn with compassionate love and justice,
> to turn inward and find holy fire at the core,
> to turn outward and see the world that is all
> of one flesh with us...

A Dreaded Disease and Two Dramatic Plays

"People avoid me as if I have a virus," Linda claimed, "a virus that people believe could easily infect them." I was oblivious to this strange disease at the time, didn't recognize it when it struck. In retrospect, Linda seems to have gotten it right. I didn't realize how people were reacting, so I didn't believe it. Linda saw it clearly:

> I seem to have the most unusual effect on people—they visibly move away from me and begin to speak—if at all—in a very quiet voice. I hate this. I think there should be a course on how to deal with people who are grieving. My situation might be threatening, but I am not!

Grief stalked us everywhere, haunting our daily lives, staving off friends and strangers, emerging suddenly in unexpected places. I am sitting behind a young man in a crowded plane on one of our flights rushing across the sky that first year. He casually chats with his girlfriend next to him. I think little about them; it's all empty talk to me, white noise brushing across my ears. But then I notice the back of this young man's head, the soft curl of his hair, the light brown color, the way it hangs down loosely just off his neck. His talk is deep as it penetrates my body now, seeping into the marrow.

I look at Linda sitting next to me on the plane, reading quietly. Suddenly tears begin to roll down my warm cheeks as I listen to Jonathan's voice, so clear and compelling as we stream across the heavens.

Jonathan was everywhere. That would always be true, at least as long as I mapped my story onto the other stories played out in the world. Like the first time we went with our friends to see a play at Trinity Rep in Providence after Jonathan's death. We attended the theater with these friends several times each year before Jonathan died, but it took a long time to trust anyone after his death. To go for a light dinner or to a dramatic play with anyone was an extraordinary commitment.

That particular night, we saw Eugene O'Neill's *Long Day's Journey into Night*. I should have known better, since I was familiar with the play. It draws you through a long and dark journey of drug addiction, a family nightmare, jolting in its implications and in its force, "a play of old sorrow written in tears and blood," O'Neill himself had said. We followed the tormented journey that night, fixed in our chairs in the dark theater, watching the characters drift across the stage, as their lives unravel and the illusions of meaning fade like the muffled blast of a foghorn in the morning mist. Leaving the theater, out in the brisk air, silence walked with us along the sidewalks. We sat glum in the backseat of the Volvo stationwagon as our friends quietly drove us home.

A few months after seeing that play, though, like Linda, I was able to work through such moments with some sense of regained balance. As Linda put it, after we saw another play at Trinity:

> *Though* Angels in America *is a play about death, AIDS, and horror, there is humor in it too and I was surprised at how much I enjoyed it. I don't think I could have sat through it several months ago without thinking about Jonathan the whole time. In one scene, the lover of a man dying of AIDS left him because he couldn't bear to watch him suffer—it was too threatening to his own self. The man hated himself but could not help staying away. It made me think of those people who have avoided contact with me since Jonathan's death and I understand now that they just don't know what to do. They feel threatened. Yet I can't forgive them for their cowardice.*

Journey into Night and the Hebrew Bible

We remained torn by contradictions that first year. How could it be otherwise? It was much the same during that last year of Jonathan's life, a year that contradicted everything we knew about our normal young man on the stairs.

I live through that final year over and over again, not as a repetition compulsion but to discover still another perspective, deepening my journey now into my own dark night. Unlike Linda's, my thoughts about Jonathan ordinarily don't take me to the last day of his life, though, nor do I feel our last visit with him was upbeat.

I was worried about Jonathan when we saw him in San Francisco that last time, and although I wanted to find promise in his recovery, there were many signs—his irritability and impulsive flashes thinly veiled by a calm and mellow style, for example—suggesting his struggle for survival was ongoing, like ours, his victory far from secure. Linda wanted to believe otherwise, and so did I. Somehow she was able to. Her journal suggests the fear and the hope we both shared, but also the difference in our perceptions through the first year of mourning:

> I have two visions in my head. One of Jonathan, reasonable and at peace in San Francisco. He is getting better, happy, almost content. But, then, I cannot help imagining him after the overdose, lying on his bed, alone, in his small apartment on Nevada Street. I am tortured by the thought he might have been afraid, that he knew what was happening but could not get help. I am told a heroin death is a peaceful one and I hope with all my heart this is true. I hope this vision will subside one day and the other vision will remain.

For me, neither vision captures the Jonathan I knew. He had a Messianic hope, a Jewish yearning for the Promised Land, a belief in a perfection not yet arrived. He was in exile, seeking home. It is a Jewish trait: a longing for something more, a desire creating a restlessness and dissatisfaction with what is. Jonathan ran into a false Messiah, not Bar-Kochba, David Alroy, or Sabbatai Zevi, but something just as enthralling and slick.

It was bad luck. It could happen to anyone. The seduction by drugs is a pull we can all get caught in. Some are more susceptible to it than others. Jonathan was one of those particularly wired for the seduction. Others are drawn to less dangerous, more acceptable, forms of attachment and obsession. But we can all be charmed and spellbound—bewitched, allured by the whistling wheel whirling with the wind of fascination.

Yes, it could happen to any of us. It is our story. We are not immune to the seduction. We cannot claim this story will not happen to us. It does and it has.

Addiction is never uncomplicated. It is like life itself. And it is like death. That, of course, is the problem. None of us escapes. But the death of a child is particularly painful and tragic. It defeats all reasonable expectations. We wish we could have prevented it. We feel guilty we didn't. We are caught.

But we are obligated to survive.

This is what King David knew, the Biblical text tells us. And these texts too are important in my pursuit, necessary for survival in exile. They call to all of us, I believe.

King David's infant is sick, the text tells us. The king fasts, lying on the ground as if he is in his grave already, mourning his lost son. But then, hearing the report of his child's death, David surprises his servants, rises from the ground, calls for food. Stunned, the servants ask David about this sudden reversal of behavior. How can he get up and eat, weighted down by such tragic news?—we all wonder.

"But now he is dead, wherefore should I fast? Can I bring him back again?" David responds. "I shall go to him, but he will not return to me."

Is David numb when he says this? As a father, he claims he has done all he can. He needs to get on with his life. His son will not return to him.

Yes, I see his point. I consider it carefully. Yet I can't believe it.

But there is another story; there always is in Jewish tradition-another text for all of us to think about. It is about David's adult son, Absalom, not an infant but a full grown man with whom David had a long and difficult history. Absalom—rebel, thorn in David's side, murderer—leads a plot to take control of the kingdom from his father. He is conspiring behind his father's back, betraying him. Understandably David is distraught.

But what does the father say when he hears from his messenger that his son has been killed, the rebellion put down? What most fathers would say, what I would say: "O my son, my son Absalom! If only I had died instead of you!"

I believe that. Who wouldn't? We cannot do much about the life or the death of our adult sons, but we would die instead of them.

Why did David react so differently to the loss of these two sons, though? I want to know.

King David had developed a significant history with Absalom, I imagine, a long male relationship, a deep bond as father and son. Yes, like Jonathan, Absalom was not a baby. He was a mature man, grown and shaped under the shadow of his father. They knew each other's heart beat through the cadence of time. Perhaps that made a difference.

I would have died instead of him.

At the Jewish Deli

These Biblical stories speak directly to us if we choose to listen, and, for the same reason, I love to hear people talk about Jonathan now. Sitting around a table on holidays, I yearn for people to tell stories about him, picture him for me. It was not always like that. Right after Jonathan's death, the best stories entered my body like a bullet. I would wilt, almost collapse at their telling.

I am sitting with my mother, eating a sandwich on a hot summer afternoon, thinking about all those long, narrow delis with formica-top tables and plain wooden chairs, a meat counter on one side, protected by tall, slanted glass—like the Carnegie Deli in New York. I can smell pastrami in the air.

"I remember taking him to Buttonwood Park near our house when he was young," my mother starts. "It would be early in the morning, and Jonathan would be waiting on the back porch after breakfast as I put the dishes away in the kitchen. There was a cool breeze there.

"Let's go, Grandma," he would insist. "We don't have all day, you know." And then we were off, walking through the neighborhood across Hawthorn Street, down the path in the woods bordering the park, over to the zoo. He loved the buffalos. 'Once they came right up to the fence and tried to spit on my Dad,' he told me.

"After the zoo, we'd get in the car back at the house and drive downtown to the Whaling Museum. As soon as we got inside, Jonathan always raced over the wooden floors to the model whaling ship, explored it from top to bottom. He loved to climb all over that boat, down beneath the deck. And you could count on him to have questions for the women who worked there.

"Pardon me," he would say, looking up at them as they stood behind the counter. 'Pardon me, but do you know what time the Seaman's Bethel is open?' 'Pardon me, but could I go over to the Mariner's Home and take a look around?' He always had questions, needed answers."

My lost son remains with me, although he is not visible in the expected places. Be assured he is here, though, very much a part of the world. It is unfair when people remain silent, refusing to name him.

Memory, stories, tradition—all strengthen the bond between parent and child after death. They keep Jonathan close to me. I am not sure I can make any difference to him any more, but he continues to make a difference to me.

Even if King David was right, that our sons will not return to us, we can still return to them. My relationship with Jonathan continues to grow and change. He is alive for me, a part of the family.

> I listened, motionless and still;
> And, as I mounted up the hill,
> The music in my heart I bore,
> Long after it was heard no more.

The Headstone of Memory
and the Language of Grief

*I*t is not that I need to be told, but Marge Piercy reminds me:

> *We are the people of the book*
> *Through fire and mud and dust we have borne*
> *our scrolls tenderly as a baby swaddled in a blanket,*
> *traveling with our words sewn in our clothes*
> *and carried on our backs...*
> *We must live the word and make it real.*

I agree. The text is our life, flexible and tolerant, living protection against the hard stone of death. Words reach out to wrap us in their warmth, to remind us of our connection to family, to the human community. We travel with words, like angels, sewn in our clothes. But words can also disturb us, cut deep into our flesh, turn violent, even with good intention, when we demand comfort, not probing.

Listen to the mourner, the Jewish tradition tells us. Wait on his silence.

Yes, it is to tradition that I must look now to discover myself, where I am. We are the People of the Book, burying our dead, carrying our scrolls "as a baby swaddled in a blanket."

> *We are going to order the headstone on Wednesday and it is almost unbearable to think about it. I cannot seem to get out of the routine of feeling good one day and awful the next. I know that being out and doing things makes me feel better, but I actually find myself counting the minutes until I can return to the safety of my house. When I arrive home, I go straight to my comfortable chair in front of the TV and wrap myself in the comfort of mindless shows. For me, now, this is safe. The outside world can't touch me.*

Yet I cannot help but think about Jonathan. Will I ever really realize that he is in fact gone? I don't know. I guess I will always just think of him as being 26.

It's true. Jonathan is frozen by time now. He will never be older than 26, and I will never hug and kiss him again, hear his hearty laugh, celebrate another birthday with him. He will never get married, never give us grandchildren, never captivate us again with his funny duck walk, his sonorous voice, his electric style.

∽

In our house in Dartmouth, I get up from the granite table in my study, hard like the stone of death, and pace aimlessly over the Berber rug, blue and gray, cushioning my feet. I wander near the shelves of books lining the walls. Suddenly I see a title there, *Tough Jews,* by Paul Breines. I snatch the book from the shelf, open it slowly.

A Father's Day card is tucked away between the cover and the first page. "Happy Father's Day," Jonathan has written. "Thanks for all of your help these last few weeks trying to find me a job. I can feel that big oppurtunity [sic] coming up any day now. I'll keep you posted. I love you, Jonathan."

I tenderly turn the first page. There's another note from Jonathan: "6.19.94 Father's Day '94 For a great dad, a great friend, and one of the toughest Jews I know. In my eyes you are truly an 'ubber [sic] mensch'! Thanks for all of your help and guidance! I love you! Jonathan."

It is his voice coming off that page. I hear it clearly. "Deep love is stronger than life itself," a Jewish proverb tells us. I see what the proverb means now. Deep love reaches beyond the grave. "Deep love is thicker than blood."

But what if our children die before us? How then do we fulfill the covenantal promise?

∽

*When Israel stood to receive the Torah, God said: "I am giving
you my Torah. Bring Me good guarantors that you will guard it."
The Israelites said: "Our ancestors will be our guarantors." This
was not acceptable. The Israelites spoke again: "Our prophets
will be our guarantors." This was not acceptable. But then the
Israelites, newly freed from the slavery of Egypt, said: "Behold,
our children are our guarantors." God accepted. "For their sake, I
give the Torah to you."*

Only our children can keep the promise. Like the original covenant,
a deeply shared story binds us together, but what is the meaning of
that story when the guarantors die before their time? Who will keep
the story alive?

~

When Jonathan lived in the halfway house in New York, he told
me he was reading an interesting book about the magic of stories. "It
reminded me, Dad, of those stories you used to tell me at bedtime,"
he said. Later, I discovered by chance the same book while browsing
through the lonely stacks of the university library, seeking comfort,
thinking about Cowboy Jonathan. It was called *Better Than Life*, written by Daniel Pernac, born in Casablanca in 1944, the same year I was
born. In it, Pernac had written:

> *At first we were thinking only of his pleasure. His early
> years had put us in a state of grace. The absolute wonder
> of this new life endowed us with a kind of genius. For him,
> we became story-tellers. As soon as he could understand
> language, we told him stories. We didn't even know we had
> that skill. His pleasure inspired us. His happiness made
> us inventive. For him, we created characters, added on the
> chapters, refined the suspense....*

Yes, reading a story every evening fulfilled the finest
function of prayer, the most impartial, the least
speculative, the one that touches only the human kind:
the forgiveness of trespasses.

Pernac is right. Storytelling creates wonder. Reading a story to your innocent child fulfills the finest function of prayer, like the forgiveness of trespasses.

But, like broken glass, the death of a child cuts sharply into the magic of story, refusing the promise of a natural and coherent life. We lose the thread of the story, a part of our name, of our given identity. We need now to create a future out of the loss, out of the jagged shards of memory buried within the rubble. We need to give the loss itself an identity, a habitation, a new home to live in. We struggle to find language for our grief.

Grief has become our story, grief is our prayer.

Discovering Tradition Amidst the Rubble

I find another book on my shelf, a storybook about the Biblical Jonathan, best friend to David before he became king. I used to read the story to Jonathan when he was very young but have not looked at it in a long time. Opening the cover, I come across a handwritten note from two close relatives, dated May 15, 1969, about three months after Jonathan was born.

> To Jonathan:
>
> May this great hero inspire you to read about other heroes in the Bible.
>
> With love, Harold and Susan.

I am sure the story, filled with friendship and brotherly love, inspired Jonathan when he first read it. He must have thought of the story when he was growing up with his brother Jeremy. It is the way we weave story into story, threading our life into meaningful narrative if we dare.

These stories illuminate patterns deep in the rubble, giving the gift of perspective. We need to pursue them deep into the interior self, our own shared wilderness.

~

Just after Aaron, the brother of Moses, was appointed High Priest, he sees his two children killed by God for offering "strange fire before the Lord," the Biblical text tells us.

Commentators remain baffled to this day. Why did it happen? How could God murder Aaron's two sons? Some say the sons were careless, not taking their priestly functions seriously enough. Perhaps they had gotten drunk, some suggest. But one Talmudic scholar, when asked why we mention these deaths on the Day of Atonement, claims: "It is to teach us that just as the Day of Atonement effects forgiveness for the children of Israel, so does the death of the righteous effect forgiveness for the children of Israel."

The implication: "The righteous suffer most when evil is rampant, and their suffering and death stir people to bethink their way, and to move toward penitence by resisting evil in themselves and in the world."

So Aaron's two sons were righteous. Perhaps they came too close to God in their desires. This perspective suits me. I put it on like a rich garment.

Was Jonathan righteous?

Yes, I believe he was.

Despite the death of his two sons, though, Aaron didn't waver in his resolve. He continued to do good deeds, preparing for his high responsibility and purpose as the newly appointed High Priest, obeying, like Job, the commandments from God. He didn't make a fuss, didn't complain, went on with his work.

But his silence weighs heavily on us.

"And Aaron held his peace," the Biblical text insists.

Wrestling with Angels,
Holidays and Graduation

*H*olidays fall from the sky like stone. They are particularly hard because holidays are a natural time to call for stories, connecting the living with the dead, giving memory a spiritual dimension. And such memories are always family memories, a rustling murmur shared by our son Jeremy as well, recalling a beloved brother, protector, confidant, an older friend lost in time.

The first Mother's Day after Jonathan's death was excruciating for Linda:

> *It is Mother's Day today. We are going to see Jeremy. I am thinking about how Jonathan always liked holidays and it makes me sad. I don't know how I really feel today—I guess no worse than any other day. I think I have been so saturated with Mother's Day by the media that it really doesn't make much difference. I told Jeremy I would not be celebrating Mother's Day this year and his response was, "You are still my mother." He's right. He must be feeling so abandoned. He wonders: "Am I an only child?" He is not, I tell him. He will always have a brother.*
>
> *Well, I am going to try to make this a pleasant day for Jeremy—his graduation from Tufts is next week. Why do I always feel like I should make it okay for others? Well, Jeremy did say to me "You are still a mother." And I have to remember that I am. He is terrific and we are lucky to have him. I am enraged that he has to deal with this horror at such a young age. I want to protect him from it. I want him to be okay, happy, successful in his life. What mother wouldn't?*

Jeremy is making heroic strides in his own battle with loss. Each milestone in his life makes us proud, but Jonathan is not here to mark the celebration, share in the wonder of accomplishment. At the end of

Jeremy's graduation from Tufts in May, nine months after Jonathan's death, Linda connected the joy of Jeremy's college graduation with the despair of the unveiling of Jonathan's tombstone:

> Jeremy's graduation is over and it was both wonderful and sad. Bittersweet, as they say. We are so proud of Jeremy. To be able to finish his senior year of college during this excruciatingly painful year was a true accomplishment. He is quite a guy. I love him so much.
>
> My parents were here for the graduation and for the week following, but as soon as they left I went into a deep funk. I guess I didn't have time to think about it when they were here. My next hurdle is the unveiling and that's driving me crazy. I wish I had not invited all of Jonathan's friends. They are not replying and Bob wants to start calling them—that would be too much for me. I feel that would make it into a party atmosphere. I am disappointed we heard from so few of them—maybe they will just show up. I am a bit sorry we are doing this—it would have been easier if we had just gone and done it—the three of us. I cannot believe I actually am thinking about what food to serve—it is beyond my comprehension that we are planning this ritual. I still believe Jonathan is out there somewhere—I wonder if I will ever totally accept his death.

A few days later, feeling the necessity to communicate with Jonathan, Linda wrote a letter to him.

> Dear Jonathan,
>
> We are getting closer to the day of the unveiling of your stone and I cannot believe that I am just going along and planning it. If I really thought about it and what it really is, I know I couldn't do it. I have talked to many of your friends—they have finally started to reply—Christine and Jim Henson in the past two days. They miss you so much, just like we do and they really did love you. They all tell me what a wonderful person you were and how much you

always helped them. I wish you knew that and could have imagined your life sober. I know you thought your life would not be worth living without drugs, but you were so wrong.

We miss you so much....Jonathan, we love you so much and I don't think I will ever truly accept that you are gone. You will always be my son.

Love, Mom

Part Five

Cowboy Jonathan Remembered

I need to fit some of the fragments together.

It is as if Jonathan lived three lives.

First, Jonathan growing up, the normal young man, the bar-mitzvah boy, wrapped in his new tallit, poised and self-possessed on the bima at Tifereth Israel Synagogue in New Bedford, talking about *tikkun olam,* leading the congregation in prayer; and the schoolboy caught on video going to the prom at Dartmouth High in his tuxedo, red bow tie, and stiff black formal shoes, a beaming and reluctant smile for the camera, next to a splendid girlfriend with flowers pinned to her white dress, one of many young women drawn to him as he was drawn to them over the years; and the college undergraduate, in cap and gown, bermuda shorts underneath, dirty sneakers on his feet, a rebel celebrating the ritual of academic success at commencement exercises in the university football stadium at Amherst with family and friends; and the graduate student and organizer, in working clothes, on the picket line with labor groups, joined in the endless struggle in the street for social justice, economic reform, solidarity.

Second, the Jonathan wrestling with drug addiction, the normal young man no longer there, restless and uneasy, moving from one institution to the next, hospitals and halfway houses, trying to figure out how to spring the trap he had caught himself in. He is at Butler, then with a blood infection at Miriam in Providence, then a pastoral retreat at Hazelden. He briefly considers living with two girls he knows who want to take care of him in White Fish, Montana, not far from the rushing waters of the Big Black Foot River, but instead returns from Hazelden to enter the Fellowship House in gritty New York. Then the West Coast. Palm Springs. Finally, the hills of San Francisco.

And forever now, the Jonathan of memory, the Jonathan who will always exist for me in that mythic place between father and son, the scholar gypsy, Cowboy Jonathan.

Linda sees it differently though.

On February 9, 1967, Bob showed up at the door of my apartment on Commonwealth Avenue and we were together more than apart until our wedding day, June 25, 1967. We celebrated our marriage accompanied by a huge thunderstorm at a reception under a big tent on my parents' lawn.

Then, two years to the day after our first date, February 9, 1969, Jonathan came into the world, our world then. It was like a dream. Magic. He lit up our lives. That first warning call on July 17, 1994, from the mother of Jonathan's friend, informed us that our son, Jonathan, had a serious and potentially fatal disease—heroin addiction. At 4:00AM on August 20, 1995, we received a second phone call that completed that roller coaster ride and changed our lives forever: The San Francisco coroner informed us that our son had lost his battle with the disease and had died of a drug overdose. Our days between those two calls were filled with hard work, horror, denial, anger, tremendous fear, struggle, guilt, torture, and even, at times, some hope. Our whole family shared all of these feelings, and Bob, Jeremy, and I are left remembering that year.

The Curve of Grief in Contrast

The first year after Jonathan's death was the second year of the disappearance of the Jonathan we knew best. Although I went back to work as an academic administrator, I soon resigned that position and returned to the English department as a professor. As the Jewish sage Shemayah, in the midst of the Roman Empire, put it in the *Sayings of the Fathers*: "Love work; hate lordship; and seek no intimacy with the ruling power." Gladiators in the forum are not models for Jewish manhood. Shemayah's words make sense to me.

The daily routine of driving to my office, greeting my staff, talking with colleagues and friends, kept me upright during that first year, but the work seemed cramped, too much of the surface, too close to the bureaucratic values of efficiency and control, pushing and manipulating from the outside. Rubbing shoulders once again with colleagues in the English department might inspire me, root me back in, offer a more careful investigation of the interior self, I hoped.

"I had a dream last night, doctor," I tell my psychiatrist one morning in her small office. "I'm walking on what appears to be a series of surfaces layed out like floors at different levels, like an Escher illustration or a Piranesi drawing, planes leading nowhere and everywhere, staircases coming to an abrupt end. It makes me dizzy. If I look down from these surfaces, it's unsettling, endless, an abyss. I'm trying to get to a bed, soft and comfortable, located in the middle of all these surfaces. The bed is beautiful, illuminated, the source of a radiant light. It has a white canopy with four posts."

For Linda, the first year was different. It was important for her to take it slowly, to let the ordinary world return in small pieces. I could not have done it the way she did. But she remains convinced it was the best way for her; she needed shelter from the storm.

When I look at my "situation," I seem to be outside of myself. I still wonder how parents can survive the death of a child. I am not that person because I was not supposed to be. I always pictured my life as being one that would go very smoothly, with things fitting into place. These kinds of things happen to other people. I often think there is something wrong with me because I expected things would be so much better by now. But well into the first year, I still don't know if I know for sure that Jonathan is gone. I sometimes feel the whole thing is a dream, and I guess that is because I went through last year in a semi-daze. The fog seems to be lifting, but I find it impossible to believe I can live out the rest of my life knowing the reality of it all. I am panicked over the thought of returning to my classroom as a teacher, but I think once I get into the swing of it, things will go okay.

Bob believes our grief actually began the day we found out Jonathan was probably addicted. In thinking about it, I know this is true. It was the first time in my life I felt so powerless; I felt I was out of my body. I will never forget that feeling and since then I have felt it over and over again.

The first year after Jonathan's death I was in a daze. Everything was a first without him: first birthday, first holidays, first Mother's Day, first Father's Day. Last year on this day Jonathan was alive. I did not know that Jonathan was dead; I could not say that Jonathan was dead. I could not feel that Jonathan was dead, I believed the whole nightmare would soon be over. I kept thinking, "I have paid my dues and now make Jonathan come back." I did not go back to teaching and stayed home because I could not face the world. Most people—especially Bob and my mother—believed I was doing the wrong thing, but I know now it was the only thing I could do.

I stayed involved with a few committees at school and joined the board of a city-wide committee comprised of people who worked for agencies helping addicts. They did a lot of good work, and I felt I was there in honor of Jonathan. But mostly, I sat home and tried to let reality in a very little bit at a time. I watched old movies and television shows, and I cleaned a lot. My house was never so clean. Mindless activities helped me get through the day.

I waited for the mail and read the letters that filled the mailbox. They held kind words and compassion and came from people that I knew and some I barely knew at all. I often read them over and over, especially those from people who had experienced the death of a child in their own family.

I waited for the call from Jonathan saying it had all been a terrible mistake, that he was alive and strong. When I went out, I counted the minutes until I could return to the safe haven of my house. If the light on the answering machine was blinking, I would often think "It must be Jonathan." But then I would remember. I talked to people when I could, but I often did not answer the phone.

When I meet parents who have just lost children and they think they are going crazy, I tell them anything they think and feel is normal but they must let the shock of reality in very, very slowly.

⁓

In a book on the Jewish mourner's prayer, Leon Wieseltier wrestles with the Biblical and Talmudic notion that the sons acquit the fathers but the fathers cannot acquit the sons. This interests me.

We rejoice when a father helps a son, cry when a son needs to lift the father. But that is in this world, when the father is still alive. In the Jewish tradition, the oldest son is required to say the *Kaddish* for his father when the father dies, in part, the commentators claim, to help the father's soul make its way from earth to heaven. The son helps there. But can a living father help the soul of a son whose body lies in the grave?

That is a more difficult question. Wieseltier pursues it, finding a telling commentary deep in the Talmud, focused on David's lament for his son Absalom, the adult son, the one he shared a significant history with, the one shaped under the shadow of the father:

> And the king was much moved, and went to the upper room above the gateway and he wept, and as he went he said, O my son Absalom, my son, my son Absalom! would God I had died for thee, O Absalom, my son, my son!...The king covered his face, and the king cried in a loud voice, O my son Absalom, O Absalom, my son, my son!

The rabbis want to know why David says "my son" eight times. It is not simply a mathematical question, nor is it strictly mystical. It is a question to help gain perspective. "Why?"—the ultimate question about the mystery of human life. I want to know how others have responded. I read on.

> Seven times, for the seven levels of Gehenna (the underworld) from which David raised him; and as for the eighth there are those who say it was to restore Absalom's head to his body, and there are those who say it was to bring him to the world to come.

So, as Wieseltier concludes, the fathers can indeed acquit the sons. David's cry here is not a lament but a prayer.

Yes, I embrace the notion; it seems exactly right: Grief is our story, grief is our prayer, grief returns Jonathan to his home.

The Classroom

*T*he second year I went back to work, and most of my energy was spent walking into that school where Jonathan had been. He had walked those halls—his footprints were there. I was afraid to leave the math department area and if I had to leave it, I counted my steps as I returned. I watched the faces of the other teachers who looked at me, sometimes with pity and sometimes with fear. Many just turned away and did not look at me at all. Some said kind things about Jonathan and told me they were sorry. There were others who knew Jonathan, had him in their classes, advised him through his four years of high school, who never said a thing. Others, who had had Jeremy in class, did not ask about him. Did they think he was not involved in this whole tragedy? It was hard to be there, and by the end of each day I was exhausted.

The students were actually much more open and less afraid to offer kind words. If it had not been for them, I would not have been able to continue teaching. I tried to limit the number of after-school committees I committed to and tried to make my life as simple as possible. I had changed; I was a different person. I sometimes think I should have changed my name when Jonathan died. When people looked at me, they thought they were looking at Linda, but they were looking at someone different. By March, I requested a three-week leave. I needed time to reorient myself, to get a better sense of who I had become.

Like most parents, I had sat behind schoolroom desks, in the evening at the close of day, listening to Jonathan's teachers offer periodic reports from the front of the class, had watched him play basketball in the school gym with its smell of stale sweat, had smiled proudly with the other parents in the auditorium when he was awarded his school letter as co-captain of the golf team. But, yes, for Linda, a teacher in that school, it was different. It was an act of courage to return to those tiled corridors and metal lockers that second year.

Linda loved the classroom and teaching, and she loved her students, sometimes bright and uninhibited, sometimes frustrating and bullheaded. Unfortunately, teachers rarely get the opportunity to focus their energy and time exclusively on teaching anymore. They are expected to be everything to everyone, caregiver and disciplinarian, entertainer and bureaucrat, parent and friend. Teachers have become the scapegoats for the problems in public education today.

After Jonathan's death, it would have been to everyone's advantage to give Linda an opportunity to simply go to her classroom and teach math. She would have found renewed purpose in that. Instead the administration and the bureaucracy kept eating away at her.

I could see her drifting, distancing herself from any substantive connection to the school. She began to focus elsewhere, although she remained removed from most matters. She was clearly a different person than she had been before Jonathan's death.

Heroin and the Rabbi

*H*ow much did Jonathan's death from heroin, in particular, shape our grief and our behavior, our longing and desire? How much did it shape the response from those around us? Not only the brutal fact of his loss but the implications of heroin as the instigator of that loss need perspective. I want to know what Jonathan was thinking when he was high on heroin, how he felt when he became self-reflective about it, how it affected his relationships with friends and acquaintances. For a while after his death I thought I should try heroin myself, to find his pain in the recesses of my own body, to see the world as he saw it. It was a haunting idea. Some of the Romantic writers would have understood it—Coleridge and Poe, DeQuincey.

I didn't go after it.

Jonathan was ashamed of his habit, humiliated by it. I know he feared he might never be able to break his addiction. But I want to know more. Some will insist I am still in denial when I say this, but I resist the notion that he should have felt shame. His addiction had nothing to do with that. His fear I understand.

To me there was something courageous in his struggle. He was wrestling with demons that few of us dare confront. His journey was closer to the bone than most, more authentic in its refusal to compromise with ordinary life. I never thought this was shameful; I only regret he did not make it through.

I never aimed my rage directly at Jonathan. He was trapped by demons bigger than he was, battling to beat them—both the drugs and the flat life that surrounded him. He yearned for something more and then got caught on the way.

For me, it was never a question of when Jonathan might hit bottom. How could it be? There was no bottom, only the challenge of creating meaning in the depths of the abyss. How could I be upset with him for trying to meet that challenge?

You say that's too romantic, even sentimental? It cuts too close to the worst of pop culture, the wrongheaded worship of cultural icons like Hendrix and Joplin, Garcia and Cobain? Yes, I know Jonathan had been intrigued by this kind of pop culture. I should have realized how fully saturated the music scene was with the weight of hard drugs and death. But it was not pop culture that seduced him, unless it was the emptiness itself that sucked him in, the shimmering moon glow of fragmented dreams and desires wrapped in flickering images on the screens of marketeers, advertising masquerading as show business, fraudulent alchemists, wholesale magicians mirroring back our emotions, for sale or for lease, consumed in the neon wilderness.

There must be a future with depth, something more than we have created for ourselves in this image-obsessed age. Blake and Wordsworth warned us of this long ago. Otherwise, we too are caught and trapped, defeated by the dogs of cynicism, by the grubbing for material goods, by the addiction to fun and endless entertainment, country clubs and speed boats, videos and shopping, the sensation and thrill of the new.

When an orthodox rabbi visited Jonathan at the hospital in Providence, he advised: "Wrap the sacred tefillin around your forearm, it will carry more power than the heroin needle you push in there. It will protect you and heal you deep down." The black leather boxes of the tefillin hold sacred parchment with selections from the *Shema*, the Jewish prayer of faith: "Hear O Israel, The Lord Our God, The Lord Is One."

The rabbi was saying that if Jonathan listened closely he would find something stronger than the force of heroin. As the *Shema* indicates, Jonathan should hear those words of faith, "Bind them as a sign on your hand." He should make them part of his flesh, his home, seal them, with all his might, into his heart, into his soul, as the prayer directs.

According to Jewish tradition, the *Shema* consists of 248 words, in harmony with the 248 parts of the body. That is not by chance.

The rabbi, firm but gentle, offered us all an alternative, an opening taking us beyond the charming world of sensation and image making.

He was explaining a ritual, like circumcision, that reconfirmed a way of marking tradition on Jonathan's flesh, a way of joining the communal story of Judaism, body and soul, a way of rejuvenating the story of the covenant, a story that Jonathan knew in the recesses of his body, that I knew in the same way, that my father knew before me, and his father, and Abraham, Isaac and Jacob long before.

Like the idea of mitzvot, obedience to the commandments, the tefillin wrapped around Jonathan's arm was a way to defeat the carelessness of the world, an ancient reminder of how freedom is bound to responsibility. The tefillin beckoned to discipline and prayer, to a belief in caring. It claimed that what we do cannot be based on casual and thoughtless opinion. If we are to achieve our human identity, created in the image of God, we must acknowledge that everything we do makes a difference. Otherwise we worship false idols.

Jonathan was trapped by a false messiah, seduced by false idols. But we should remember him as a passionate fighter for social justice, not as a dope fiend; as a bright and determined rebel, not as a social misfit. Jonathan had depth, grappled for meaning. He always did, whether on the picket line or on the drug-filled streets of New York. I am not angry about that. I give him credit for it.

Yes, most people still hold negative images of drug addiction, especially heroin addiction. I understand that. Believe me, I do. But to deny Jonathan's involvement is to deny part of his life and to misinterpret its meaning. Some will say such denial serves a reasonable purpose. I disagree.

Discovering a Voice

*A*t the end of this first year back teaching, I decided that a scholarship in Jonathan's memory should be presented to a graduating senior at Dartmouth High School. So many people seemed to have forgotten Jonathan and the fact that he had walked these halls for four years. I needed to say his name and tell the wonderful things he had done. When I told Bob I wanted to set the scholarship up, he wondered who would present it. I knew immediately I would be able to do it. It would take great courage, but I felt it would be healing to stand in front of people and talk about Jonathan. So the first Jonathan Blake Waxler Memorial Scholarship was established at Dartmouth High School. Kristi Maso, a graduating senior who had spent many hours promoting social justice, would receive the first award. That night, Bob reminded me that he would be in the front row, waiting to take over if I could not go on. But when I stood up to talk, I took a deep breath and a wonderful feeling came over me. This was a chance to talk about my son. As I began to speak, all eyes were on me, many filled with tears.*

I can still hear Linda's voice that night, near the end of the second year after Jonathan's death. From my place in the front row, I looked up at Linda as she approached the podium from her seat on the stage. No tears, no wavering. She walked with a simple sense of pride and dignity. It was as if she were giving birth again.

"My son, Jonathan Waxler, graduated from Dartmouth High School in 1987 and from UMass Amherst with a bachelor's degree in political science in 1991 and with a master's degree in labor studies and education in 1993. In his brief 26 years, Jonathan helped organize community groups, worked with labor unions, campaigned for educational and social issues, taught a course

at UMass Amherst on labor history, had articles that he wrote published, and in general worked tirelessly to improve the lives of people less fortunate than himself.

"When he was working for the United Electrical Workers in the fall of 1993, my husband and I attended a dinner with Jonathan, his colleagues, and several of the workers he had been helping. One woman told me she wanted to meet Jonathan's parents because as she put it: 'Jonathan has changed my life. With his help, my dignity has been restored.'

"Jonathan died a tragic death on August 20, 1995. Words will never express how much I, my husband Bob, my son Jeremy, our family, and all of his friends miss him. We will forever have a hole in our hearts. When his friends from all over the country gathered at a memorial service to celebrate his life, each one spoke about how much Jonathan had enriched their young lives. Jonathan lived only for a short time, but during that time he gave to others all that he had. He knew the meaning of giving, and so he touched more people in his short life than many do blessed with a long life."

～

The response the next day was heart warming. People came to tell me how moved they were by the presentation and they did indeed remember Jonathan and often thought about him. These were the people who had turned away when they saw me in the hall and walked the other way. I would present this scholarship for three more years but finally stopped because the person in charge of the awards ceremony decided to make it as hard as possible to present the award. There will always be those whose cruelty will astound me.

Reading, Writing and Arithmetic

*L*ike Linda, I too had returned to teaching, and by the end of the second year, still knotted and troubled, I was trying to talk with students who often reminded me of Jonathan at that age. I too had turned a corner.

Linda was a mathematician, someone who pursued abstract forms, geometric shapes of perfection. It had always been crucial for her to hold onto something permanent, something that did not change, something beyond the flux and contingencies of life. Abstract numbers served as a protection against the onslaught of mortality, the liquid flow of life in the flesh. Now there was nothing between her and the grave. This must have contributed to that ferocity and bitterness, that anger that was so much a part of her.

It was different for me. The study of literature made it different. Language called me to its sensuous texture, like flesh itself, evoking desire, reminding me of loss, whenever I was willing to enter it. Reading great literature, I had always been swimming in a sea of mortality, whether I was aware of it or not.

Literature helped keep my anger in check. It gave me a sense of imperfection, of proportions, of tolerance. But it didn't foreclose on passion, nor did it serve as an escape from Jonathan's death. Sometimes, standing in an empty room, I will yell out loud at Jonathan, even now, and wonder why this tragedy happened. "Why, Jonathan, why?" I shout at him, then patiently wait, in the silence, listening for his reply.

But I can't find the fierce anger Linda feels. Maybe it's still too deep for me to connect with. What I do know is the feeling of loss will never end. That's the contradiction and the truth of the healing process, an endless sorrow mellowing with time.

Nevertheless, by the end of the second year, Linda and I shared more in common in the synapses of our mental landscape than we realized. We were both beginning to reform ourselves through the silence of a voice we could only imagine, and we were both returning to the classroom eager to unearth some comfort and energy there. There would never be closure for our grief, but we were together, looking for a place with a permit to reinvent our family.

We needed a home.

The Akedah and the Labyrinth

*T*he beginning of the third year after Jonathan's death I began to settle in as a faculty member, working on an anthology about the *Changing Lives Through Literature* program for Notre Dame Press and teaching graduate and undergraduate courses at a normal clip. The linen shroud that had hung tight over the world seemed to be lifting, but I couldn't yet get a steady grasp on the world spinning without Jonathan.

Jeremy had begun law school at Suffolk University in Boston, and although I didn't want to invest too many of my own dreams in him, I admired his endurance. I lost sleep before every law exam he took, agonized about any possible setback he might suffer, phoned him frequently just to hear his voice, drove my car through the chaotic city streets to see him without the slightest reason or cause.

"Let me take a look at that brief you're writing for class," I implored. "What about those cases you've been reading?" I questioned. "How's the internship at the public defender's office going?" I wanted to know.

I needed to protect him from trouble just as I had needed to save Jonathan.

You say I hadn't learned to let go. You're right. Perhaps I never will. But I continue to work on it. As I have said, a father is obligated to protect his sons. I realize others believe such obligations can turn to an obsessive need for control. But it is a difficult line to draw, the distinction between protection and compassion. The boundaries are not always clear. When do you stop sacrificing for the one you love? How rigid should the geometric lines be? To what extent is it our obligation to make sure the promise is fulfilled?

Wasn't this Abraham's dilemma when he made that destined journey in Biblical times from Beer-Sheba to Moriah, from the ordinary to the extraordinary? A father, he must have been in agony, struggling with the sacred call to give up his son. How could he let go of Isaac, the promise itself? Should he give Isaac back to God, let him return to his origins? Isaac was the gift God had given to him and Sarah, his wife. But didn't the father have an obligation to protect his son? What kind of God demanded such things from His children anyway?

Sarah does not go on that journey with Abraham up to Moriah. Neither did Linda, I imagine, although surely her journey was just as harrowing.

Some commentators say that when Sarah hears that Abraham plans to bind and sacrifice their son, she cannot bear it. She dies from the violence of grief, broken-hearted, buried in the cave of Machpelah, they claim.

Linda survives, though. I am grateful for that.

But why doesn't Abraham argue with God? Where is his anger at this apparent injustice? I cannot find it. His silence is stunning, if not baffling, as father, with knife and fire, and son, shouldering the wood of sacrifice, journey for three days over the rocky terrain to Moriah. Although Abraham tells his servants that the two, father and son, will return together—"we will worship and we will return to you"—Isaac will not return with Abraham.

Something extraordinary happens, though. "On the mount of the Lord there is a vision." A ram, his horns caught in the thicket on this new year, replaces Isaac on the sacrificial altar. Thank God. Isaac is let go, free to marry Rebekah under the family tent, free to become a husband and father. The covenant is secure; the promise kept:

> Because you have done this and have not withheld your son, our favored one, I will bestow My blessing upon you and make your descendants as numerous as the stars of heaven and the sands on the seashore; and your descendants shall seize the gates of their foes.

That is what I want for my sons. Jonathan and Jeremy. What father wouldn't?

～

Yet the brutal facts of the past cannot be rewritten, only atoned for. If our children are the guarantors of the covenant, of the story, then without them, what guarantees do we have?

I will always wonder if I could have built a stronger bond between Jonathan and myself, one that would have held him tight to this world, pulling him from the seductive power of heroin, just as I wish the power of the *Shema* had beaten the heroin needle.

Jonathan's death was not my death though. And I need to remind myself about that continually just as I need to consider Jeremy, alive and fighting, flesh and bones above ground, in the midst of the rubble. I cannot lie down in the grave.

～

I am reminded of another story, about the Biblical Jacob. Do you recall it? When he heard his son Joseph was dead, thrown into a pit, torn to pieces by a savage beast, Jacob "rent his clothes, put sackcloth on his loins, and observed mourning for his son many days. All his sons and daughters sought to comfort him; but he refused to be comforted saying, "Nay, but I will go down to the grave to my son mourning."

Jacob, weighted down with grief, was like so many fathers, ready to join his son in the grave. It was as if the father and the son had both fallen dead in the pit. It's as if Joseph's death would have been Jacob's as well.

In this story, though, there's a twist. Joseph turns out not to be dead. Instead Jacob travels down to Egypt to see him, to be with him. The father goes down to Egypt not to identify a corpse but to find his son returned to him.

Yes, the father travels to the city to see his living son. I ride to Boston to see Jeremy. But that's not an adequate balance for me. It can never be. One son doesn't substitute for another in life or death.

Unlike Joseph, Jonathan will not return in this ordinary life. Nothing is ordinary anymore, though. In fact, every ordinary moment of my relationship with Jonathan while he was alive, typical relationships in so many ways, is now utterly mysterious and extraordinary. His death is my life; his life, my death. But I will not lie down in the grave.

We have crossed the limen into the uncanny. We are at Abraham's visionary moment at Moriah. "In the mount of the Lord it shall be seen."

As the French poet puts it, thinking as much about life as about books, as much about death as about language: "The book is a labyrinth. You think you are leaving and only get in deeper."

We are like the blast of the shofar on the Day of Atonement, rams caught in the thicket.

A Shock of Recognition

*D*uring the third year, Linda was destined to find a new life, if she could, in a much more communal way than I was. She worked hard to connect with new friends, to seek new relationships, and to head up a search for a new house to live in. Her journey was more radical than mine, more wrenching to the body, more demanding, more insistent on the necessity for new possibilities. Her path was harrowing and distinct, filled with thickets all along the way.

The professionals claim each of us mourns differently. I believe that is true. But a warning from Jewish tradition seems appropriate here: "Whoever wants to mourn more than the law requires must be mourning for something else."

Linda's recovery work needed to proceed along its own path, but it was bound to exact an exorbitant emotional and physical toll on her and on those around her. Ironically she saw it as an improvement on her life.

The third year was a little better, but it was still hard to believe the whole ordeal would not be over soon. I was tired all the time, and my life was bewildering. There were still times I was afraid to leave the house. I was angry, sad, lonely, and still overwhelmed with grief. I guess I knew this was going to be a part of my life forever, but I still held out hope, I suppose, that I would somehow regain my old self.

Somewhere in this year, there was a shock of recognition. I finally knew that Jonathan was dead—I could say the words. Of course, there were moments I would still allow myself to believe he was alive. But I was slowly accepting the inevitable. I knew that Jonathan's spirit would always remain on this earth with me, Bob, and Jeremy. It would remain with his family and friends and with all those people he touched during his short life. Little by little I found myself feeling some of the old good feelings. They would creep up on me when least expected.

The Big Apple and Wedding Bells

*T*he poet Pinero put it this way:

New York City sunday morning means
liquor store closed
bars don't open 'til noon
and my connection wasn't upping
a 25 cent balloon...
but sunday morning in New York City
for the junkie there ain't no pity
we just walk the streets with loaded dice
and hear people say there goes miky
miky pinero
they call him the junkie christ

Yes, I remember going for breakfast across the street from the Roosevelt Hospital that morning when Jeremy and I picked up Jonathan to take him to LaGuardia for the last time. It was Sunday, streets nearly deserted, the homeless, like gypsies, sleeping against the walls. No pity. Just walking the streets with loaded dice. I wasn't sure I would ever be able to return.

But there had been other times in New York. Good times. As a young boy, I had gone to the Big City with my parents, stayed at the old Manhattan Hotel, seen *My Fair Lady* with the original cast, looked out over the majestic skyline from the top of the Empire State Building, listened to the drum beat and watched the go-go dancers from the sidewalk in front of the Metropole.

And Linda and I had spent a New Year's Eve in Times Square watching the silver ball drop, taken Jonathan and Jeremy to their first plays on Broadway, shopped up and down the avenues, browsed through the galleries in Soho, haunted the clubs in Greenwich Village. Once we had loved New York, its vitality, its taxi horns and police whistles, its pastrami on rye.

We had not been back to New York City since Jonathan's death. We had tried to go back once, in the spring of 1995, while Jonathan was still in San Francisco, but had to leave early because Bob was so distressed. So many awful incidents had occurred in New York before and after Jonathan was in treatment, and Bob had witnessed them all. But in the spring of 1999, we thought we would try again. We could always leave at a moment's notice. We stayed in a location different from other visits but did our normal routine—plays, museums, restaurants, some shopping. And we found ourselves having a good time! The old demons did not seem to be lurking around each block, and we were careful not to go to places with too much memory. The best part was knowing we would be able to return again without the fear.

Weddings were another fear. How could I watch young people Jonathan's age getting married, knowing it would never happen for him? But in the fall of 1999, just four years after Jonathan's death, my best friend's daughter, Debra, got married. I had known Debra since she was a toddler and loved her. Her mother, Shelly, and I had been close friends for many, many years and were more like sisters than friends. Our two families celebrated holidays together and were there to support each other through good and bad times. She was always there for me after Jonathan died and mourned for him with me. I wasn't very involved in the planning of the wedding. Under different circumstances, I would have been. In the end, though, I thanked Debra: "I felt joy again and it was because of you." There were tears in our eyes when I told her.

For Linda the recognition that Jonathan was dead and the ability to celebrate a milestone of a very dear friend marked out new boundaries of the self. A funeral and a wedding, an end and a beginning, a narrow grave plot and a wedding huppah open to the sky, Isaac bound for sacrifice and Isaac unbound for marriage and fatherhood: a scaffolding with balance.

But the loss of Jonathan has about it the sense of an ultimate collapse, and although the wedding rejuvenated Linda it had a different texture, a more liquid and temporary effect for me. It couldn't balance the permanent disappearance of our first son. We would both agree on that.

Making Progress: The Life of the Mind

*T*hrough the third year into the fourth, I continued to work the talking cure with my psychiatrist in her threadbare office, wrote a short essay for the *Brown Magazine*, weaving memory and story in the space left by Jonathan's absence, and completed work on the *Changing Lives Through Literature* anthology for Notre Dame Press. I felt connected through the cadence of language, close to convincing myself there was virtue in the concerns of human consciousness. It was part of my Jewish identity. As the imagined voice of Jewishness puts it in a Kenneth Koch poem:

> ...But
> Why not admit that I
> Gave you the life
> Of the mind as a thing
> To aspire to?

I don't doubt there is meaning in such a life, human freedom discovered through the work of the mind, but, in retrospect, whatever meaning I felt then came not so much from the life of contemplation itself, from the beauty and purity of its process, but from the pride of accomplishment, the products of achievement. I felt engaged and useful, accountable, efficient, and in control. I was wrong to believe I had found a way out, although I was finding a way in.

Helping others and myself, I had yet to discover the hidden places of loss, the secret hideouts harboring the fugitives of forgotten desire. I was creating a cover story, a thin cosmetic makeover, distancing myself from the sorrow at the bone. When the Brown University editor called to tell me he wanted to publish my article, he noted over the phone that I had left out the cause of Jonathan's death: "The readers will want to know how he died. You have to put it in."

I felt uneasy about that at first, resisted the idea, but eventually saw his point. "It will help people to know," he said.

And although I wrote a loving tribute to Jonathan, Cowboy Jonathan as I called him in the introduction to the *Changing Lives Through Literature* anthology, I never hinted at his lost battle there. I needed the protection, but I also knew I needed to grapple with the sorrow and with the guilt looming like death ready to erupt close to the bone.

I went to the local jail for several literature sessions with criminal offenders during this period. It was a cold and bloodless place. Steel doors slamming shut. Empty spaces echoing the meanness and misery of metal traps.

I sat with the offenders, my students, around a long table in a small room packed with books tumbling off the shelves—the library, a place for liberation, I thought. Almost all of these men were substance abusers. Some were heroin addicts. We talked for several hours about "Sonny's Blues," a story by James Baldwin about two brothers, an algebra teacher (the narrator) and a jazz musician (and heroin addict), Sonny himself.

It was the best discussion I've ever heard on that story. "Yes, I know how Sonny felt," they told me. "Sitting alone in that jail cell, he must've craved a visit from his brother." Their voices ached with longing and loneliness, with compassion and need, with tough insights into life on the streets, addiction and regret.

As the narrator in the story says: "I felt my guts were going to come spilling out or that I was going to choke or scream. This would always be at a moment when I was remembering some specific thing Sonny had once said or done." I was uncertain how much I could take in that jail before I was broken.

"I'm not sure I can go back there," I told Linda one time.

"Then don't," came her practical Talmudic response.

Linda was protecting herself too. Acknowledging that Jonathan was dead, she was now less ferocious and bitter in her approach to life than she had been, less closed off from the world. It was as if she had let

Jonathan warm her heart finally, hoping her voice would shape a loving place for him in the world. It was a way of integrating the loss of Jonathan into her new life, cautiously, little by little, one piece at a time.

She was becoming a teacher in an entirely new context, an authoritative voice resonating deep within her.

Yet her life since Jonathan's death had never been easy or straightforward. It was as if she were always traveling on two roads at the same time, getting better as she got worse, gaining health and confidence as she unraveled, fell apart. She was coming to terms with Jonathan's death, gaining some distance, but now the emotional turmoil seemed to intensify her physical pain, move her closer to the horror.

Though she had found a new voice, strong and deep, she remained physically and emotionally troubled, a bilious presence at times, diagnosed with fibromyalgia by a world-renowned physician in Boston, suffering pain from head to toe, headaches, stomachaches, backaches. She was crampy and in continuous heated arguments with her school administrators. Her body was betraying her, but from her perspective she was making steady progress:

> During the fourth year, I finally realized, Jonathan's death was something I would live with for the rest of my life. The second week after Jonathan died, a woman who had also lost a child came up to me and said, "You will never get over this." What a fool, I thought. Of course I will get over it. No one could feel this pain their whole life. But though her timing was very poor, she was right. I could see that. His death and the pain it brings has become an integral part of my life.
>
> I had avoided the thought of Jonathan in a casket, buried in the ground. When it came into my head, I shook it out. But now that his death was real, I found it hard not to think about it. The thought that his body is gone, a skeleton only remaining, is impossible for me to accept. But I know now that that is not all that is left of my vibrant, life-loving, smart, and beautiful son. Truly, it is not.

A Practical Application

N ear the end of the fourth year, Linda wrote her own article about grief, a stunning composite of her feelings and her knowledge. It was published in several places, including the *Providence Journal Sunday Magazine*. She was stretching, touching others, rejoining a community, becoming a writer of her own life. As she noted in her journal:

> I was convinced that so many of the things I had been thinking and feeling had to be written down. It was my sincere intention that the people who read the article would be helped in some way.

Her voice was authentic and strong, like the time she stood up to address the Dartmouth High School crowd, but now the audience was wider, and she had a different lesson to teach. It was a gift Jonathan had bequeathed to her, a need to give back. The article, filled with good advice, received a warm response from its readers. Many friends and colleagues at the university remarked on it, sought me out, wanted to talk about it.

"It's fresh and original," they said. "It made me pause, think."

"It helps mark a cultural shift," a science professor explained to me. "Instead of focusing on the deceased, we should focus on the survivors. I'll remember that."

Many more spoke to Linda directly, perhaps believing that the strange virus she caught when Jonathan fell ill was no longer a threat to them. Here's the article with its ordered list and plain style, practical advice for all of us.

> No one is ever prepared to approach and talk to a bereaved parent. And no parent is ever prepared for the death of a child. It is our worst nightmare; we believe it is unsurvivable.

Our son Jonathan died in 1995 at the age of 26. For a long time, I have been convinced that many of us need training in dealing with parents who have lost children. There are so many misconceptions and fears. As a result, people tend to avoid the parents thinking, "I don't know what to say." Not only do we have to deal with our overwhelming grief but also with people avoiding us and friends abandoning us. It's almost as if our grief is contagious. So I am prompted to document some important points with the hope that readers will be better able to deal with friends and acquaintances who are living this nightmare.

1. *Grief is not really a process that one goes through a step at a time. Grieving is a roller coaster ride and it is circular. The first couple of years, we are numb. When the numbness goes away, we are shocked to see that the world has gone on without our child. When we come out of this numbness we are new people, slowly beginning to adjust to what has become our "new normal."*

2. *We are parents without the right number of children. Adjusting to this could take years. Some of the emotions that grieving parents feel are fear, anger, guilt, sorrow, loss of future, isolation, abandonment—these are not steps that we work through but feelings that come back over and over again with different intensity and in different forms. There really is no "closure."*

3. *When a parent loses a child, his heart is literally broken. A huge hole is left. This hole will never heal—only the jagged edges around the hole may heal with time. Our grief, not always in the same form and maybe not as intense, will be with us the rest of our lives.*

4. *It does not matter how our child died, whether he was one week old or 60 years old, or if we do or do not have surviving children. The loss of a child is an act against nature. The right order is that a parent should die first.*

5. *It takes a long time for most grieving parents to accept the fact that their child is dead. We can only allow the truth in a little at a time. This may take years.*

6. *Bereaved parents are no stronger than anyone else. We survive for many reasons. We may have other children; we need to be there for our spouse and other family members; we may feel that if we die, our child's memory will die with us; but mostly we survive because we see no other choice. We loved our children with all our hearts, the same way any parent loves a child. It is not because we loved our child less that we survive.*

7. *What you say is not important—the important thing is to say something. Ignoring a bereaved parent is only adding to her burden. Just ask "How are you doing?" And, when a bereaved parent returns to the workplace, make sure that you stop by once in a while just to say "hello." Remember, our "new life" is just in the infancy stage and it is a very difficult road ahead. Our grief is forever.*

8. *Call the bereaved parent just to let her know you are thinking about her. Don't be insulted if the person does not call you. For years after a child dies, there are many days when the parent just does not have the energy to pick up the phone. Grieving is not only difficult but saps most of a person's energy for a long period of time. Letters are helpful also. Most grieving parents appreciate those letters more than you can imagine.*

9. *Some people are afraid to mention our child's name because they will "remind" us of our sorrow or because we might cry. You will not remind us because we never forget; we are living it every minute of every day. And don't worry if we cry; we will stop. You might want to cry a bit with us. We want to talk about our child. Mention his name. One of our biggest fears is that he will be forgotten and one of our biggest joys is to hear his name.*

10. *Everyone grieves differently. There is very little a bereaved parent does or feels that is not within the normal range. We seldom ask for help but if you listen and watch carefully, we will give out signals that will show what we need.*

11. *Never think that a grieving parent is holding on to his grief. We do the best we can and we move along as fast as we can, but it is hard work—probably the hardest thing we will ever do.*

12. *Remember, there will always be certain times of the year that will trigger immense sadness and overwhelming grief. Birthdays, anniversaries of the death, holidays, Mother's Day and Father's Day, weddings and funerals are just some. We can never prepare ourselves for these days. Sometimes they end up being easier than we thought they would be and sometimes harder. A simple "I am thinking of you and I know this day must be hard" goes a long way with bereaved parents.*

Can you help? Yes! One thing you can do, besides being there for support, is to contact Compassionate Friends, a wonderful organization that forms groups of bereaved parents around the world. Here a parent can find comfort in the fact they are not alone and their feelings, no matter what they are, are shared by other members of the group. We learn we are not insane—our feelings are normal for bereaved parents. We cry together, but we also laugh together. Ask for information about the group and offer to go with the parent to the first meeting. With the help of this group, I am becoming a new person and I am working hard on adjusting to my "new normal." I can no longer see my son's face except in pictures or hear his voice except on a family video, but I am beginning to realize that Jonathan's being and soul are nestled in the hole in my heart and that for as long as I live, he will be with me wherever I go.

The return of Jonathan after his disappearance appears to amend King David's notion that our sons will not return to us. The lost may be found. But I wonder what a phrase like "new normal," adopted from the language of the recovery community, actually means. To acquire new friends, compassionate because they have suffered pain similar to ours, invites comfort. Yet such friends are continuous reminders of our loss, of where we have been, of where we are. I will always regret that reminder just as I regret that Jonathan had to spend the last year of his life with companions suffering the same pain that he suffered.

It was part of the dilemma we found ourselves in during that fourth year—the need to find a new place, to seek new friends, to talk about the extraordinary loss that separates us from the rest of the world, all knotted together with the wish that we were not separate, that we were simply ordinary, common like everyone else.

The "new normal" is only temporary. It speaks to what we are missing, what we lack. It doesn't return us to what we had, nor does it allow what we had to return to us. It fails to provide muscle and bone. I still believe that.

Part Six

A New Home and a Family Reframed

*A*s the fifth year approached, Linda and I moved into a new home, brand new, overlooking a wooded valley that changes as the natural seasons change and offers a brilliant sunset any evening we choose to sit outside on our extensive wooden deck and look to the west to admire it. Linda invested her time and energy with the builders when we first bought it, focusing her attention like a laser beam on the project. Her sweat and anxiety made it a success.

The house looked beautiful when we were done, with its wonderful sense of expansive space, walls stretching two floors high, a balcony peering down to greet us from above. And Linda continues to create an aesthetic wonder from room to room.

We bought paintings and rugs, soft easy chairs and long wooden bookcases, granite tops and stunning lamps, all in an effort to find peace and comfort. We also placed a mezuzah on the right front doorpost, as we have in each house we have moved into. The mezuzah is a parchment with two paragraphs from the *Shema* placed in a small metal box. "…And you shall write them upon the doorposts of your house and upon your gates." It is similar to the tefillin, with its two leather boxes, wrapped around the arm and forehead of a Jewish man in prayer.

The project helped draw Linda through sorrow, giving her an opportunity to be productive, to feel accomplished. It offered a clear path for leaving the old world behind and gaining a new one. And, most important, Jonathan's presence was woven through it all, from rosebushes to photographs.

At the same time, Jeremy discovered Nicole, who came from Ohio as if on a sweet breeze, looking for a job in marketing in Boston, fresh out of college. She dazzled him, as he dazzled her. They quickly became inseparable, friends noting an aura radiating from their beaming smiles wherever they went. Nicole cared about Jeremy, just what he needed. "A gift from Jonathan," Linda would say.

We had a brunch when we moved into the house, celebrating Jeremy's graduation from law school. It was our coming-out party, and we invited about 140 friends, old and new. It worked. That Sunday morning our house was packed with people enjoying an assortment of bagels, cream cheese, lox from New York, melon soup, exotic salads, scrumptious quiche, pecan rolls, chocolate croissants, all on plates dancing with bright color. The house brimmed with warmth, the rooms overflowed like beakers of laughter. We sipped mimosas, drank cool wine, talked, shook hands, embraced. We were transported. And everyone noticed Linda that day.

"The sparkle is back in your life," they said. "We can see it." Had destiny once again turned our lives around?

The new house was not far from the old one. It was time, and we were ready. We discovered that wherever we went Jonathan would go with us. We were sad to leave the beautiful, tall, graceful pines he planted in the backyard and the yellow rosebushes he planted for me one Mother's Day. But we planted another yellow rosebush right outside our new door and it bloomed this year through November. Oh yes, Jonathan is with us. We think of him as we look out over the beautiful valley of trees, a view that brings us peace in our new home. He's out there and in here—with us, always.

The Soft Music of Tears

*F*ive years since Jonathan's death. When I look back, I see that my life has two distinct parts: before Jonathan's death and after. I am a totally different person, and when I catch a glimpse of my old life I smile and am happy for it.

I am here, though, and that's important. It was so hard to reread what I had written in the early days because there is so much agony. My first instinct was to protect myself and throw it all away. But it is a part of my life. It has reshaped me. Little by little, I have grown into a new person. In one sense, Jonathan is almost more a part of my life now than he was before. That may sound odd, but when your children are grown, doing well, happy, you think about them with pleasure but not constantly. Jonathan is now with me all the time, and so many things trigger my thoughts of him through the day.

Of course, I still sometimes wonder if the message on the answering machine might be him, or I think I see him on occasion in the distance. Sometimes, when I am in a supermarket, I stop and smile. I now walk easily down the aisles, not afraid that someone I know will turn the corner at the end. For so many of the past five years, I was afraid to be in public places, to see people I knew, to talk small talk, to see people happily going about their everyday lives when mine was basically stopped. I was afraid that the music coming over the speaker system would make me cry or that I would see food on the shelf that had been a favorite of Jonathan's. I actually went, for years, to a market across town to avoid some of these threats. What progress I have made!

I seem to be crying a lot lately. I can be anywhere, doing anything, and I just begin to cry. The tears just stream down my face, as if they are disconnected from me. But it is a different kind of crying. It is not that heart-wrenching crying I experienced the first several years—the kind of crying you think will never end—the kind that leaves you exhausted and empty. This crying is soft and sad. The difference is that I know I will be okay when it stops and will simply go on with what I am doing.

Opening the Heart to Ghosts

*T*he cautious Dr. Watson once asked the detective Sherlock Holmes why he risked drug abuse, and Holmes immediately responded:

> My mind rebels at stagnation. Give me problems, give me work, give me the abstruse cryptogram, or the most intricate analysis, and I am in my own proper atmosphere. I can dispense with artificial stimulants.

But heroin is not a stimulant. It is, as William Burroughs claimed, "a way of life." Heroin is derived from opium, first cultivated in Southern Mesopotamia along the Tigris and Euphrates rivers by the Sumerians, who called it "the plant of joy," over 5,000 years ago. Those are the same Sumerians, by the way, generally credited with the invention of writing.

It was not until 1874, though, that a British chemist, C. R. Adler Wright, discovered heroin. Fourteen years later, the Bayer Company introduced it over the counter as a cough medicine. A year later Bayer gave us aspirin. Considered a dangerous drug, it could only be obtained with a prescription.

Today more than a million men and women, most of them young, suffer heroin addiction.

And what of the United States government's War on Drugs, based as it is on shutting down the supply, not the demand? Helicopters and border patrols, special teams crashing into warehouses, high-speed shootouts—that's what fascinates people, charms them, casts a spell—images offering rapid sensation and intrigue. But such images don't hint at a thoughtful solution. Dealers are easily replaced by other dealers, but those caught by the demon of drugs need treatment. Break the cycle of demand and save lives—that seems worthwhile to me, an approach used for a while back in the early 70s until the federal government lost its courage and suffered a failure of moral will. As Allen Ginsberg put it in 1976, "The simple basic fact is that, in cahoots with organized crime, the Narcotics Bureaus were involved in under-the-table peddling of dope, and so had built up myths reinforcing criminalization of addicts rather than medical treatment."

~

Sometimes I think about Jonathan's last night in San Francisco, wondering why it couldn't have been otherwise. Why wasn't Jonathan's roommate there to help him? Why was he alone in the apartment? I have read that an injection of naltrexone or naloxone can stop heroin from flooding the brain stem and so prevent death. Someone should have been there to revive him. I only hope, as his respiratory system began to shut down, as his breathing stumbled and failed, that he eased his way through it, without terror and without pain, with comfort and peace. I know I am near blasphemy when I suggest this, but I hope his death was as easy as the traditional death of Jewish martyrs, as easy as removing a silk-like strand of hair from fresh milk.

An offender in the *Changing Lives* program put it this way while talking about his first encounter with heroin in the late 60s. He was on his way to the gym on the MIT campus in Cambridge when he spotted a young man pleasantly sitting on the green grass. "When we came back three hours later, he was still sitting there, so blissful, so at peace. He hadn't moved. I decided whatever it was that he took, I wanted it. I wanted to be at peace like that."

DeQuincey, the nineteenth-century Romantic prose writer and friend of Wordsworth's in the Lake District, said something similar the first time he fell under the magic enthrallment of opium: "...here was the secret of happiness, about which philosophers had disputed for so many ages." For him now, "peace of mind could be sent down in gallons by the mail coach."

~

I went to Jonathan's grave recently because a friend of mine had died and I attended the funeral. My friend was a pleasant man, a gentle physician, a mensch loved by hundreds. He was 55 years old, died of cancer just as his father had died before him, and his brother and his only son.

I wanted to say something comforting to his mother after the funeral as I looked in her weary eyes, wondering how anyone could bear such anguish. Another son stood next to her, contemplating, I imagined, how long it would be before this genetic coding, run wild through their family, would attack him like a crazed terrorist.

There was nothing I could say that would make any difference. Everyone was telling her the truth, that her son had improved the lives of countless numbers of people, that he had been a good father and a loving husband, that he had lived a productive life. I knew it was important for her to hear this, but I also assumed that after listening for an hour or so such words had probably become as numbing for her as dry dust in the tomb. Telling her about Jonathan might help, I thought, letting her know she and I were part of a special community sharing the pain of parental grief. But, in the end, I didn't mention it to her. I doubt my story would have brought her peace in this life.

Only silence seemed appropriate, the same silence I felt standing at Jonathan's grave after her son's funeral. I regret Jonathan died before he could use much of his talent and potential. This is part of the tragedy of losing a child before he has come into his own. My physician friend's mother knows that feeling, I am sure, although her son was an accomplished man at 55 years old, a man who discovered his talents.

But then another friend died, the fifth year after Jonathan's death. He was in his 40s, had spent half his life in jail, haggard and disheveled when I first saw him, a heroin addict. He came into my *Changing Lives Through Literature* program in 1993, two years before Jonathan died, and turned his life around. After the program, he was determined, eager to stay away from heroin and prison. He became a student at the university, pursued his education, returned to his apartment in New Bedford each night dreaming about a college degree.

The story of his life was heroic to me as he fought his demons, demanded his purpose, pushed ahead to meet his new desires. He wasn't an accomplished scholar, didn't adjust perfectly to the rigorous discipline of university training, but whenever I saw him, I was thrilled, convinced that, although there would be slips, nothing could stop him from achieving his goal.

There was not much difference in age between us, he thought of me as a father figure and mentor. I never mentioned Jonathan to him, but I would often think about Jonathan when we talked, joined together in pursuit.

He died of throat cancer, a month or so after his mother lost another son. A few weeks before he died he came by my office at the university, left me a note that he had been there. I didn't realize it at the time, but he was making a special effort to thank me and to say goodbye. His battle was with his body, not his soul. It is the body that betrays us in the end. He remains with me, a man who did not live out his full potential…but how many of us do?

A Survival Kit

*T*hey say that couples, like branches on a family tree, often break apart after the death of a child. I have looked closely at the statistics, and the numbers do not support this belief. It is apparently an urban legend of sorts. But it's true we grieve deeply and alone in so many ways, and our grief can so weigh us down that we do not pay adequate attention to our loved ones.

I have also read that we mirror the sorrow of our spouse, sharply reflecting the pain, forcing each of us to look away from the other. I don't believe this is true either. I saw Linda's pain. I wanted to reach out to her in any way I could. Her pain was mine.

Fortunately, Linda's confidence continued to grow during the fifth year. Rooted in her own struggle, she was now convinced she should create a survival kit for others, orderly, tucked in, numbered. She was right. And she did. Here it is:

> *How have I survived?? I often wonder about that. I stand outside of myself and say, "How is this person still living and breathing?" I am amazed it is me who has gone through this excruciating trauma and come out on the other end, a changed but whole person. Here are some reasons that come to mind.*
>
> 1. *I am sure Jonathan would not forgive me if I stayed in that place of constant sorrow and deep pain. He loved life and wanted everyone around him to love life with him. My re-entry into life has been with Jonathan by my side, coaxing me slowly but surely.*
> 2. *I must go on and do things that keep Jonathan's memory alive. It gives me pleasure to give a social justice scholarship in his name at the university, to work on the board of an organization that battles addiction, or simply to help newly bereaved parents at Compassionate Friends. It gives me pleasure to talk about*

Jonathan to people who knew him and to people who did not. It gives me pleasure to remember Jonathan and to think about all the wonderful times. All of this keeps his memory alive.

3. I am still a mother and must show Jeremy that our lives, though changed, will go on and be productive and happy. He too will help keep Jonathan's memory alive and will carry the happy memories of his brother with him forever.

4. Parental grieving is hard work and takes a very long time. It is a job forever. It zaps your energy and strength and makes you feel like you are going crazy. The world goes on, but you are outside of it and for you the world has stopped. I often feel that I got off the spinning world for three or four years and when I slowly inched my way back on everything had changed. I felt like I was in a foreign country. But life pulls you back in, and you find yourself feeling some of those old feelings of joy. Maybe they are not as intense as before, but they are there.

5. Before Jonathan's death, things just seemed to work out. Our life was on a good path, we were lucky. When something was particularly worrisome, it seemed to turn out okay. I looked around me and saw tragedy hitting other families, but I was sure that it would not hit ours. Now, after Jonathan's death, things are different—I am different. Certainly, my priorities have changed. I understand that much of life is out of my control, and I do not worry as much. Other things are just not that important and must be addressed with much less thought. I think I am a more compassionate and less judgmental person. I am more patient. I know, if I am feeling sad and stuck, this will change and will get better. When I was at the beginning of my journey in this new life, I did not think I would ever come out of the darkness.

6. Time does help. Our pain gets less intense and more manageable. We learn how to manage the bad times and take advantage of the good. We learn to accept the sadness of holidays and

special occasions and how to appreciate the gift when we are surprised by joy. We learn how to put the pain and sorrow away and take it out in small pieces rather than all at once. We learn how to remember the wonderful times with our children and to smile when we are thinking about them. The bitterness and anger begin to fade, perhaps to return again and again but with less intensity and for shorter periods of time. Our sorrow will never go away and we will never stop missing our children, but they are as much a part of our new lives as they were of the old, but now in a different way.

Seeing into the Life of Things

*I*t has been said before, but I will say it again: Distance created by time relieves pain, helps us discover a new geography and history of the self, but don't expect closure for such grief.

By the end of the fifth year, distance made memories of Jonathan easier to bear, sweeter in their texture and glow. The pleasure of thinking about Jonathan grew, although that pleasure was always colored, like the sunset seen from our backporch in our new home in Dartmouth, by the sense of loss, by mortality itself.

That was part of the gift Jonathan gave us, what the poet Wordsworth knew to be the mystery of human life, the uncanny ability "to see into the life of things." The memories of Jonathan blossomed like the rosebush next to our house, the same one Jonathan had given Linda on Mother's Day. Flowers appeared suddenly on a warm day, reminding us of the endless surprise Jonathan offered.

> *I am pleased to picture Jonathan laughing and happy to be experiencing the world. I can see him, sitting in the hotel in San Francisco when he saw us drive up—this to be our last visit with him—his eyes sparkling and that beautiful, broad smile on his face.*
>
> *There is comfort in the fact that people remember him and honor him—already there are two new lives carrying his name. Our lives will never be the same because of his loss, but they wouldn't have been the same without his presence.*

In the fifth year, we discovered those fugitives of forgotten desires tucked away for too long in their secret hideouts. The heart opened to the image of Jonathan before us and shivered as that image rapidly vanished like a ghost from another world. But Linda and I achieved some balance, some perspective, some appropriate distance from the turbulence of Jonathan's life.

We were like the wedding guest who listens to the tale of the Ancient Mariner in Coleridge's poem, disturbed by the spell cast by his turbulent journey but wiser now. At the end of the poem, the Mariner is gone, leaving the wedding guest to stand alone, forlorn, stunned into wonder at the vision:

> *and now the Wedding Guest*
> *Turned from the bridegroom's door.*
> *He went like one that hath been stunned,*
> *And is of sense forlorn;*
> *A sadder and a wiser man,*
> *He rose the morrow morn.*

It was not that the world had changed. It never will. But we had. The rhythm of birth and death, the cadence of the human heart, beats eternal. That music cannot be grasped.

The pain of Jonathan's loss was less immediate and intense now, our memories of him deeper. We had touched what Wordsworth, Coleridge's good friend, called "the burden of the mystery."

> *...a sense sublime*
> *Of something far more deeply interfused,*
> *Whose dwelling is the light of setting suns,*
> *And the round ocean and the living air,*
> *And the blue sky...*

Vivid moments of Jonathan's life filtered through the thin linen of remembrance as we met the dawn each morning, deepened by loss, colored by the sunset.

Admittedly, the loss still remained too real, at times, too immediate, as if his death had just occurred yesterday. It is a cliché to say death changes us forever, but of course it does. That's why it's a cliché. And that's why the pain continues to break through the surface. I hear the shouts from Linda:

In five days it will be five years—FIVE YEARS SINCE JONATHAN DIED!!! I WANT TO SCREAM IT FROM THE ROOFTOPS—MY JONATHAN DIED. REMEMBER HIM. THINK ABOUT HIM. TALK ABOUT THE WONDERFUL PERSON HE WAS AND LIVE YOUR LIFE TO HONOR THAT!!!!!!
I can't believe that five years have passed....

But there was the beginning of the return home.

Spots of Time

*I*n remembrance of the fifth year of Jonathan's death, I stood next to Bob at the synagogue and heard him say the mourner's prayer, the Kaddish, for Jonathan. Not me, I have never said that prayer for Jonathan, not for my baby, not for my child, not for my son—it is not a natural thing for a parent to do. And from there I went with Bob to the cemetery, a place I almost never go because I cannot look at Jonathan's name on a tombstone. It is not natural to see your child's name engraved with his date of birth and his date of death. I read the words engraved beneath his name: "He touched so many with his sparkle, his warmth and his love of life." It is not natural. And again I knew it would never go away.

On our way home we stopped at a restaurant to have breakfast. We walked in, talked to the owner—just small talk—and sat down to enjoy our meal. Four years ago, even two years ago, this would not have happened. I was hesitant to walk into public places, afraid I might see people I knew and have to listen to light patter, thinking only about Jonathan and my deep despair. But this time was different. I did walk in, but Jonathan was with me in his special place in my heart, part of my new life. I have read stories about people who have limbs amputated but still feel the sensation that the limb is there. Jonathan will never truly be gone—I could not bear that.

Yes, we see him everywhere, in airplanes, in parking lots, at weddings and graduations, at holiday celebrations, and in the bright eyes of his brother Jeremy. They are "spots of time," as Wordsworth called them, sublime moments that touch eternity, rainbows radiating with the fading beauty of the ordinary light of common day, daffodils dancing on the green grass in the silent meadows of our mind.

For oft, when on my couch I lie
In vacant or in pensive mood,
They flash upon that inward eye
Which is the bliss of solitude;
And then my heart with pleasure fills,
And dances with the daffodils.

Jewish tradition says we will recognize our children again after our death because they will be wearing the good deeds we enact in their name, marvelous with wonder. But we don't have to wait until our death. Good deeds are stronger than life itself. The death of our children demands our compassion.

Glimpses of a Dear Round Face

*T*hough Linda was once again finding moments of joy in life, her physical pain increased. She suffered stomach problems, gall bladder attacks, crippling migraines, exhaustion, long memory lapses. It got worse as she took more medication, went for weekly massage therapy, tried acupuncture and health foods. Five years of working through her grief had taken a toll.

Five years. Five years trying to climb out of a hole; five years in which the world has flown by and I have been left behind, five years of working harder than I have ever worked in my life just to live and be whole again; five years of watching myself and my family make progress towards being new people—maybe better people; five years to come to the realization that Jonathan will always be with me—nestled in my heart; five years to know that Jonathan will be remembered and loved by many forever—of course, Bob and Jeremy—but also many, many friends and two new lives, little boys, who will carry his name and thus his legacy into the next generation.

Although I had returned to the contemplative life of a college professor, I found the most satisfaction when I was drawn into believing, through reading and thinking, that I was participating in a conversation beyond the immediate moment, a conversation with the best minds of the past, with the best that had been thought and said, as the Victorian sage Matthew Arnold had claimed.

More than anything else, though, glimpses of Jonathan moving through the present stirred Linda and me.

Yesterday I was sitting in the car waiting for Bob to come out of the video store. A young man came out—he was about 21—with a boy of about 14—they looked like brothers—and they were chat-

ting about a CD that the boy had rented. The young man reminded me of Jonathan—tall, big boned, chunky, a small, scraggly beard, dressed as Jonathan would dress in shorts, long-sleeved T-shirt with a short-sleeve T over it, and his baseball cap on backwards. And, most of all, he had Jonathan's dear round face. He and his brother got into the car and began to back out.

A woman was walking near the car and crossed its path. I don't know why, but she walked around the car to speak to the young man—maybe she was telling him to let her pass before he backed out. Some young men might have been annoyed at the woman but this young man listened and smiled—a big, broad, warm, sunshine smile. He chatted with her for a while, all the time smiling and nodding his head.

At one point, he threw back his head and laughed—the way Jonathan did—and then he drove away. I wanted to run after him and stop him and hold him and tell him about Jonathan and how he reminded me of him, but of course he would think I was a crazy woman.

~

A woman can be proud and stiff
When on love intent;
But love has pitched his mansion in
The place of excrement;
For nothing can be sole or whole
That has not been rent.

Or so says Crazy Jane talking to the bishop in a famous Yeats poem. She is the voice of wisdom in a world turned upside down.

Creating a Text

The Jewish prayer for the dead, the *Kaddish,* never mentions death. It celebrates God, consistent with the Jewish sense of memory and the Jewish emphasis on living in this world rather than focusing on the next. As the joke goes, it reminds us the mortality rate is still one hundred percent. Life has been given to us, given to Jonathan and to us, that is the gift.

> *Five years have past; five summers, with the length*
> *Of five long winters! and again I hear*
> *These waters, rolling from their mountain-springs*
> *With a soft inland murmur.*

"We should try to write a book," Linda suggested one day while sitting in her easy chair in the living room correcting some math papers. "It would be a way of honoring Jonathan's life. Sustaining it."

Since she had been helping bereaved parents through Compassionate Friends, the idea of a book made sense, a way of extending the discussion about grief and loss. Worthwhile, but a formidable challenge, I thought. Telling Jonathan's story had considerable merit, but demanded courage and endurance. No doubt such a project had significance in itself. In the end it might be a book of questions rather than answers, though, what the French poet Edmond Jabes claimed all books were—a journey to discover identity, always falling short, slipping back toward the grave, questioning.

"When as a child I wrote my name for the first time, I knew I was beginning a book," Jabes once said.

We write seeking the name, only to be frustrated with its mystery, captivated by its awe.

Yes, the writing of a book would be a challenge. And it would surely call Jonathan's name, breathe further life into the world. The idea had magic, another gift from Jonathan. A surprise.

The turning point came in my grief process when I read a chapter on parental grief in a book called Continuing Bonds. *The author, Dennis Klass, talks about parental grief with a lot of references to Compassionate Friends. He says, "The end of grief is not severing the bond with a dead child, but integrating the child into the parent's life in a different way than when the child was alive." How true this is and how comforting. When I read this, I felt relief. I could keep Jonathan with me.*

Romance and Illumination

*F*IVE YEARS!!! *and here I am. As I move ahead, I also dare to look back. I still can't return to the first months—they are so painful. But I do remember the call—4:00*AM *on August 20, 1995.*

I remember Bob falling forward on the bed and saying he would have to call back later. I was still insisting that a mistake had been made. "I can't live," I screamed. And then I remembered, Jeremy was home, a last visit before he returned to his senior year at Tufts. He knew. He was sobbing. (Later on, Jeremy would ask if I was going to kill myself because he had heard that statement. "No," I promised, "never.") He wanted to be left alone. I only wanted to hold him and never let go. I needed to keep him safe. Bob wanted to call his brother who lived in town. "No," I begged. "Don't call anyone. Don't tell anyone. Because then it will be true."

Yes, we have traveled a distance from that raven night, acknowledged the hard granite of the grave. The linen shroud placed over the world then has been transformed into a tallit, the Jewish prayer shawl, unfurled across the blue sky. Sitting in my easy chair, I imagine now a bridegroom, as if in a Chagall painting, wearing a white linen cloak, known in Jewish tradition as a kittle, standing beneath a huppah with his bride at a wedding with roses blooming on a bright day in May.

I am amazed when I look back on what Jeremy has accomplished since Jonathan's death: Graduating from Tufts with a degree in political science, pushing paper for a year in a Boston law firm while meditating on the murmur of his own sadness, then, three years later, matriculating from Suffolk Law School, working for a year in public service for the Secretary of State, passing an excruciating bar exam, and now, just a few months ago, joining another law firm in the private sector just outside of the city.

I'll never forget the day they posted the results of the bar exam on the Internet. Jeremy must have checked the computer screen on his desk in his office overlooking Boston Harbor a hundred times that morning. Nothing was on the Web page yet. Finally, in the early afternoon, countless names in alphabetical order popped up. But only the names of those who had passed.

He must have scrolled quickly down that list, holding his breath, pensive and sweating, until he came to the "W's." Then, slowly, his left forefinger pressing the plastic key on his board over and over again, moving cautiously now, anxiously reviewing one name at a time, he saw it: "Jeremy Regan Waxler" (his middle name given in memory of his maternal great grandmother).

The phone rang off the hook in my office at the university. He was a lawyer.

I smile now, thinking about Jeremy's current success as a young attorney practicing law in courtrooms throughout Massachusetts. He loves to hear the court officers address him as "counselor" as he walks into the district courts each day, having earned that pride and respect with his brains and guts, flesh and bone, enduring.

And I love to think about the romance illuminating the setting of Jeremy's proposal to his fianceé Nicole, with a diamond ring, in a gazebo on the Boston Common, fiery with the passion of the moment.

"Will you marry me?" he asked Nicole, kneeling on both knees, trembling slightly, cheeks bright red, in the glow of the setting sun. There is courage in that, the opening of the heart to another. The beating of the blood. Such vulnerability and trust bring magic into the world—and truth, "for whatever love sees is always true."

"Yes, Jeremy, yes. Yes, of course, I will."

~

I published another article about Jonathan as well, an article about the storm Jonathan stirred up that last year and about the meaning of the bond between a father and a son. The article appeared in *The Sunday*

Boston Globe Magazine on Father's Day. I never would have done that, although I should have, if it were not for Linda's idea about a book. I am convinced, judging by the considerable and passionate response, that Jonathan's story moved many people. It resonated.

"Please know that Jonathan's spirit will always be remembered by all that knew him and now even those of us who didn't have the pleasure," one reader wrote to me.

"I never cried on Father's Day before…I made [both my children] read your essay yesterday," a father said. "Your courage and willingness to share your story is a gift to all of us who have children at risk. And the truth of your story is that all our children are at risk."

A recovering addict and alcoholic responded: "Your chilling story reminded me of what is waiting for me 'out there' if I chose to pick up again…you certainly helped this addict remember why she goes to meetings and tries to remain vigilant.…"

And in the letters section of the *Globe*, in loving tribute, Jeremy expressed his feelings: "I hope that the raw power and emotion that this article evokes will not only alert people to the dangers of heroin, but show parents and children the importance of family. I know the emotionally wrenching experience that I experienced firsthand with the death of my brother, Jonathan Waxler, has brought me even closer to my parents and taught me to love life even more."

An oil painting of Cowboy Jonathan hangs right behind my chair in the living room of our new house, just above my head. Created by Peter Sylvada, an award-winning artist in California, from images in the Globe essay, it was used as a full-page visual in the magazine. The picture depicts Cowboy Jonathan with restless innocence rushing out into the wilderness for another adventure. There's an element of danger in his journey, but also a childlike joy as the golden sun at the horizon beckons to Cowboy Jonathan through the grayish blue storm clouds. The painting keeps him close to me. It helps me return to him, as he returns to me.

Wedding

I do more things now—I went to a wedding recently and watched as a friend's son married while his brother stood proudly by. I watched as the parents posed for pictures with their two sons, and later with their new daughter, and beamed proudly at them. I ache for a picture with my two sons—grown and happy.

I smile, with tears in my eyes, as a friend who knew Jonathan only when he was very young tells me that when she walks by the Holocaust Memorial in Buttonwood Park she stops to brush the snow off the brick that has been put there in his memory. She stops there to say hello because she remembers him even as a small child so long ago. I tell this story at a Compassionate Friends meeting and a woman, early in her grief, tells me that she has written in her notebook the part about listening so hard. She too wants to hear her child's name. I hope I have helped her....

And for Jeremy another step to make his life whole again. He is ready to be married to Nicole. When we first met Nicole, I knew that Jeremy was smitten. I believe Jonathan sent her, that he knew she would help Jeremy heal. I believe Jonathan helped lead him through his courtship of Nicole and to the green grass of Boston Common, where he asked her to marry him. This is a foreign feeling for me because I am such a concrete thinker and almost always demand physical proof. I think mathematically, in steps with a logical end. But Jeremy is so happy, beaming all the time, and as I watch him I am convinced that Jonathan's presence has helped guide him to this moment of happiness.

I see Jonathan in Jeremy's dear round face now, a melding of our two sons. Jeremy is kind and loving, and I am confident that he will carry on Jonathan's legacy of justice. Jeremy once told me he would never be happy again after Jonathan died. Our lives

were so broken that he could not imagine ever putting the pieces
back together. But his recent successes in school and in passing
the bar and then finding Nicole have made his life wonderful. And
even Nicole, who never knew Jonathan, talks often about him to
Jeremy. She recently asked Jeremy if they could name their first
son Jonathan.

Linda and I continue to grieve differently, and I am not sure where the journey will lead either one of us next. Linda would love to quit teaching and dreads returning for another year to the schools. I cannot imagine retiring from the university, but wonder if I should return to academic administration or perhaps seek another faculty position somewhere else. But, like Linda, I know we have made headway against the powerful wind of dizzy despair. We are not stuck in the grave any longer, although the grave remains.

I am noticing that more and more people are talking to me,
saying hello, smiling at me. Even strangers in the stores smile and
say hello. I turn as they walk away and say to myself, "Do I know
You?! It has happened over and over again. One day it came to
me. I am different. My eyes are not as sad and the look on my face
is more open, more inviting.

~

And then it happens. Just as we had dreamt it. Jeremy and Nicole marry on May 26, 2002, in Ohio. Nicole wears sweetpea flowers on her white antique satin wedding dress because Jeremy likes to call her that dear name, and she puts an angel pin that Linda gave her inside the folds of her gown to make sure Jonathan is present before the ceremony begins.

We are at the Toledo Country Club, an old traditional club with Japanese gardens, tailored green golf course, clay tennis courts, and a grayish-brown shingled clubhouse, spacious and sturdy. Inside, the rooms are decorated with flower arrangements of pink and lavendar tulips, light blue delphinium, peach rancuculus, blue hydrangeas—all in clear glass vases, eagerly waiting for the new bride and groom.

Outdoors, under the huppah, Jeremy and Nicole stand before a loving crowd of about 165 relatives and good friends come to witness the romance from white wooden chairs, in rows slightly curved, on the fresh green lawn smelling of spring.

Judge Arlene Singer notes this is the best weather they have had in Toledo all year, a sign of the marriage to come. Then we begin.

Jeremy and Nicole exchange personal vows. Nicole reading first from beautiful flowered paper: "You have lifted me to a new level," she tells Jeremy with tears freely flowing down her cheeks. And then Jeremy, reading from a tattered yellow legal pad, responds: "You have filled a great void left by my brother and best friend."

"Sunrise, Sunset" filters through the speaker set up on the grass. As the music floats through the air on this sun-drenched afternoon, a lone boat in the distance moves silently, gliding through the sparkling water of the Maumee River running next to the club.

Beneath the huppah, I read a poem, a sparkling sapphire selected by Jeremy called "Fidelity," by D. H. Lawrence, a poem of wild love and mutual peace, concluding with these lines caught in the late afternoon breeze:

> And when, throughout all the wild chaos of love
> slowly a gem forms, in the ancient, once-more-molten
> rocks
> of two human hearts, two ancient rocks,
> a man's heart and a woman's,
> that is the crystal of peace, the slow hard jewel of trust,
> the sapphire of fidelity.
> The gem of mutual peace emerging from the wild chaos
> of love.

Finally, as the guests watch from their seats spellbound, the best man places a glass wrapped in cloth near Jeremy's feet. As tradition bids us, Jeremy steps on that glass, breaking it into pieces, reminding us that in the midst of unity and celebration there are also fragments—rubble and mourning.

That mix is central to our Jewishness.

The huppah, the new house of the bride and groom, open to the sky and water, brings the promise of "descendants as numerous as the stars of heaven and the sands of the seashore." And it reminds me on this dreamy day that after Isaac's father let him go, Isaac, the son, was married under the tent, his home. Then the son became a father.

Under the huppah, the shattering of the glass also recalls the destruction of the Temple on Mount Moriah in Jewish tradition. It is a moment of vision. We are at the very place of the akedah, the site of the binding of Isaac.

Yes, the world remains in fragments, broken, in need of repair, *tikkun olam.*

But the wedding is far from over. Out of those fragments of broken glass, that reminder of loss, comes a call to life, shouts of "mazel tov!" from the jubilant guests. The bride and groom lead the procession to the festivities inside. Mindful of our mortality, we enter the dining room embracing life, ready for good cheer and sustenance.

Linda moves across the floor dancing with the groom, in her silk red dress, earrings shaped like glittering four-petalled flowers, a pearl necklace, long and elegant, dangling from her neck, bright party shoes on her feet. Everyone watches as mother and son smile at each other, gliding to the music, Lee Ann Womack's "I Hope You Dance." Linda has chosen it carefully.

> *Promise me that you'll give faith a fighting chance*
> *And when you get the choice to sit it out or dance*
> *I hope you—dance*

They are in the light, alone, as if on stage, the crowd standing with their wine glasses near the paneled walls, admiring the two dancers from the sidelines. The guests gaze fondly at the groom, smart and handsome in his tuxedo, his round face beaming, and at the proud mother, lost in the cadence of the moment.

I too am on my feet, standing by myself at a comfortable distance, a proud observer, eyes damp. I can barely move as the music washes over me until the song ends, breaking the spell.

Later in the night, I ask the band to play, "Old-Time Rock and Roll," from Bob Seger and the Silver Bullet Band. I will ask for it not just once but twice, dancing and dancing and dancing with Linda out on the hard wood floor.

> *Still like that old time rock and roll,*
> *That kind of music just soothes my soul,*
> *I reminisce about the days of old.*
> *With that old time rock and roll.*

We experience it everywhere, sorrow and joy, silence and song, exile and home. At the Passover seder, we eat the bitter herbs in the midst of celebrating freedom from slavery. When we recite the *Kaddish* prayer, we remember the loss of our beloved while publicly praising God. At our son's wedding, we break the glass and then, alone in silence yet together in song, we move on.

Today I know at least this: If there are tears, there is also laughter. If there is a funeral, there is also a wedding. If there is remembrance, there is also redemption.

Jonathan Blake Waxler. He had passion.

Robert P. Waxler graduated with a B.A. from Brown University, M.A. from Boston College, and Ph.D. from SUNY at Stony Brook. He is currently an English professor at University of Massachusetts, Dartmouth, where he has also served as Associate Dean of the College of Arts and Sciences and Dean

of Continuing Education and Summer Programs. He is a co-founder of the University's Center for Jewish Culture, where he was a co-director for fifteen years. In addition, Dr. Waxler is a co-editor of an anthology published by Notre Dame Press based on the internationally recognized alternative sentencing program *Changing Lives Through Literature* which he co-founded in 1991. Professor Waxler has published articles in such forums as *The Boston Globe Magazine, Journal of Popular Culture, Modern Language Studies, Brown Magazine,* and *Journal of Business Communications.* He has also contributed essays to *A Mensch Among Men*, an anthology published by Crossing Press, *The Book Club Book,* published by Chicago Review Press, *Success Stories,* a publication of the U.S. Department of Education, and *Total Quality Management,* from Dryden Press. His work has been featured on NPR, in Parade Magazine and *The New York Times.*

Linda Lassoff Waxler graduated with a B.A. from Tufts University and a M.A. from SUNY at Stony Brook. She is a math teacher at Dartmouth High School and previously taught at Fisher College and Bristol Community College. During her time at Dartmouth High School, she has been very active on a system-wide math committee and on committees concerned with curriculum change. She is a co-founder of the *SWIMS* Program (Successful Women in Math and Science) and a founding member of the New Bedford Community Health Center. Ms. Waxler also serves as an active board member of Compassionate Friends and Positive Action Against Chemical Addiction.